W9-AOY-955

New Directions for
Community Colleges

Arthur M. Cohen
Editor-in-Chief

Richard L. Wagoner
Associate Editor

Gabriel Jones
Managing Editor

Contemplative Teaching and Learning

Keith Kroll
Editor

Number 151 • Fall 2010
Jossey-Bass
San Francisco

CONTEMPLATIVE TEACHING AND LEARNING
Keith Kroll (ed.)
New Directions for Community Colleges, no. 151

Arthur M. Cohen, Editor-in-Chief
Richard L. Wagoner, Associate Editor
Gabriel Jones, Managing Editor

NEW DIRECTIONS FOR COMMUNITY COLLEGES (ISSN 0194-3081, electronic ISSN 1536-0733) is part of The Jossey-Bass Higher and Adult Education Series and is published quarterly by Wiley Subscription Services, Inc., A Wiley Company, at Jossey-Bass, 989 Market Street, San Francisco, CA 94103-1741. Periodicals Postage Paid at San Francisco, California, and at additional mailing offices. POSTMASTER: Send address changes to New Directions for Community Colleges, Jossey-Bass, 989 Market Street, San Francisco, CA 94103-1741.

SUBSCRIPTIONS cost $89.00 for individuals and $259.00 for institutions, agencies, and libraries in the United States. Prices subject to change.

EDITORIAL CORRESPONDENCE should be sent to the Editor-in-Chief, Arthur M. Cohen, at the Graduate School of Education and Information Studies, University of California, Box 951521, Los Angeles, CA 90095-1521. All manuscripts receive anonymous reviews by external referees.

New Directions for Community Colleges is indexed in CIJE: Current Index to Journals in Education (ERIC), Contents Pages in Education (T&F), Current Abstracts (EBSCO), Ed/Net (Simpson Communications), Education Index/Abstracts (H. W. Wilson), Educational Research Abstracts Online (T&F), ERIC Database (Education Resources Information Center), and Resources in Education (ERIC).

Microfilm copies of issues and articles are available in 16mm and 35mm, as well as microfiche in 105mm, through University Microfilms Inc., 300 North Zeeb Road, Ann Arbor, MI 48106-1346.

CONTENTS

EDITOR'S NOTES

Higher education has historically excelled in promoting teaching and learning with respect to critical reasoning and quantitative analysis—what might be described as higher-order thinking skills. It has not always done so well in fostering the teaching and learning that develop contemplative methods and practice—the kind of learning that teaches students to be reflective, to be mindful, and to pay attention.

In describing this kind of education, Arthur Zajonc (2008), director of the Center for Contemplative Mind in Society and professor of physics at Amherst College, writes:

> Contemplative pedagogy makes conscious use of a wide range of practices for two essential ends:
>
> • the cultivation of attention and emotional balance
> • the development of faculties required for insight and creativity [p. 9].

In direct opposition to this contemplative model of education is the life and educational experience of many community college students, which can best be described as one of detachment and disengagement. Students park or get off the bus, and then walk into a building, down a hallway, and into a classroom. After changing rooms for three or four classes (a trend among my students is to take all of their courses two days a week, which then allows them to work more days), they walk back down the hallway, get back into their cars or onto the bus, and leave campus. As one of my students told me, "It's hard to balance work, school, family, and other commitments. Not a complaint, just a statement." Research on community college students supports this student's description of a harried and hurried life as typical of many community college students.

It is no surprise, then, that our students struggle to pay attention, to be in the moment, to be present. In class, they appear to be somewhere else—in the previous moment or the next moment. It is common to see students walking in the hallway talking on a cell phone while holding a conversation with someone they are walking with, or typing at a computer station while listening to an iPod and talking on a cell phone. My students laugh when I ask them if they ever read or write in silence. They respond that rather than silence, they are holding a conversation with a roommate, the TV is on, iPod buds are in their ears, music is playing on a radio, and a cell phone is held to their ear.

Moreover, in uncertain economic times, the message students repeatedly hear is that with respect to their education, speed and training are to be valued more than learning, intellectual engagement, and contemplation.

This volume serves as a source book for community college faculty, staff, and administrators interested in developing and fostering contemplative teaching and learning in the classroom and on the community college campus.

Since contemplative teaching and learning may be new to readers, the first chapter, by Rick Repetti, provides a historical introduction to contemplative practices and argues for the importance of a contemplative philosophy of education. In Chapter Two, Maria Lichtmann extends the argument made in Chapter One by offering a theoretical framework for the essential role that contemplative teaching and learning, and in particular spirituality, can have in the education of community college students.

In Chapter Three, Robert Haight introduces the contemplative classroom practices that are described in succeeding chapters. Haight reimagines the community college classroom as a *sangha*—a space that promotes cooperation, community, compassion, and civility.

In Chapter Four, Dan Huston describes how mindfulness meditation and emotional intelligence can be fostered in the teaching of communications. The role of mindfulness meditation in the teaching of developmental reading and writing is the focus of Kate Garretson in Chapter Five. In Chapter Six, Jacqueline Griswold describes the importance that contemplative practices can play in helping students in human service programs cope with the stress and burnout all too common in this occupation. Matthew Shippee, a full-time community college teacher and professional musician, describes in Chapter Seven the role of contemplative practice in teaching music.

Contemplative practice is not confined to the community college classroom. In Chapter Eight, Anne Faulkner and Guy Gooding profile the decades-long program of formation—a type of reflective practice—that was central to professional development within the Dallas County Community College District.

As several authors in this volume point out, community colleges have historically played a major role in higher education with respect to vocational training. In Chapter Nine, Kip Scott examines the root meaning of vocation, *vocatio*, and describes how contemplative practices can be an essential part of helping community college students find their calling, or life's work.

The last chapter offers a brief overview of the contemplative practices explored throughout the volume and provides specific practices that readers can begin to explore and include as part of their classroom pedagogy.

The contemplative theories and practices described in this volume, some of them ancient—for example, mindfulness meditation is thousands of years old—offer a new direction for community college teaching and learning.

NEW DIRECTIONS FOR COMMUNITY COLLEGES • DOI: 10.1002/cc

Reference

Zajonc, A. "What Is Contemplative Pedagogy?" In *Contemplative Practices in Higher Education*. Ed. Mirabai Bush. Unpublished manuscript. Northampton, Mass.: Center for Contemplative Mind in Society, 2008.

KEITH KROLL *teaches in the English Department at Kalamazoo Valley Community College in Kalamazoo, Michigan.*

1

This chapter introduces contemplative practices, studies, and pedagogy and argues in support of a contemplative pedagogy.

The Case for a Contemplative Philosophy of Education

Rick Repetti

This article introduces contemplative practices; explains how contemplative practices, studies, and pedagogy differ; analyzes the mechanics of some key contemplative practices; reviews the research on contemplative practices and learning; and ultimately argues in support of this new direction in pedagogy.

History of Contemplative Practices, Studies, and Pedagogy

To understand the historical context of contemplative pedagogy, it may be useful to see it as an inclusive outgrowth of earlier philosophies valuing process over content and depth over coverage, such as social-emotional learning, writing across the curriculum, and critical thinking. As opposed to the so-called banking model, whereby learning consists of "information deposits," these pedagogies share a fundamental valuing of what is already in the student, to be drawn out through slow, reflective attention. Whereas these other approaches focus on communication, writing, or reasoning, this approach focuses on meditative reflection, which may accompany any of the other activities. Since it is more inclusive, any arguments in support of these pedagogies accrue to contemplative pedagogy.

Meditation is ancient. Although it is universal in human spiritual history, appearing in one form or another among Native Americans and Native Australians as well as Jews, Christians, and Muslims, meditation has been

New Directions for Community Colleges, no. 151, Fall 2010 © 2010 Wiley Periodicals, Inc.
Published online in Wiley Online Library (wileyonlinelibrary.com) • DOI: 10.1002/cc.411

perfected in Asian philosophy, particularly Indian, Buddhist, and Taoist. Meditative practices constitute the bulk of not only the methodology of these Asian philosophies but also their content, with few exceptions such as Confucianism. Thus, the Asian academy has a vast history of contemplative practices, studies, and pedagogies, and the philosophies in which they are embedded are continuous from the Classical era to the present. Until recently there has been little contemplative pedagogy within the Western academy outside Classical-era schools dominated by Stoicism and related philosophies and sectors of higher learning that intersect with Abrahamic monastic institutions. Apart from some exceptional places such as Naropa University in Boulder, Colorado (a Buddhist university, only recently fully accredited) and the Integral Institute in Louisville, Colorado (which revolves around the theories of its founder Ken Wilbur, author of Integral Theory), contemplative pedagogy remained largely outside mainstream higher education in the United States prior to about 2000, when academic interest began to shift coincident with a variety of academy-extrinsic contributory phenomena.

A vast corpus of scientific and medical research on the health-promoting, stress-reducing, and other positive effects of meditation and related mind-body disciplines like yoga has been consistently developing over the past half-century. Whereas interest in meditation, yoga, and the like entered and mostly exited our collective consciousness with the 1960s, the wider culture has now embraced these much more thoroughly. Just one trend shows this clearly: *Yoga Journal*'s "2008 Yoga in America" study reports that Americans spend $5.7 billion annually on yoga-related products (classes, equipment, clothing, vacations, DVDs, videos, and literature), an 87% increase over the previous study that was done in 2004 (March 2008, p. 93).

In the academy, numerous books and journal articles on contemplative pedagogy have been published (as a glance at the lists of chapter references in this volume reveals), contemplative pedagogy programs have been implemented at such venerated institutions as Brown University and the University of Michigan, and contemplative pedagogy training seminars have been offered at competitive colleges such as Smith College. In the past decade, academics from all disciplines have begun to incorporate contemplative practices into the classroom (Bush, 2006). Perhaps the most significant academic catalyst is the Center for Contemplative Mind in Society, which, in collaboration with the Fetzer Institute and the American Council of Learned Societies, began granting contemplative practice fellowships in 1996 to support contemplative pedagogy faculty development. To date, the center has granted over a hundred such fellowships, each sparking a contemplative course or program, and it has spawned the Association for Contemplative Mind in Higher Education, which in 2009, its first year, had over three hundred faculty members. More important for our purposes, researchers are validating the effects of contemplative practices on learning (Shapiro, Brown, and Astin, 2009).

Community College Context

The Garrison report, *Contemplation and Education* (Garrison Institute, 2005), examines a variety of K–12 contemplative pedagogy programs. The positive results of this research are particularly relevant because community college students are mostly at high school or lower developmental levels. That our students are multiply unprepared is our greatest challenge. The weakening of public K–12 education, No Child Left Behind, and the erosion of other social and cultural institutions, replaced by ubiquitous text messaging and other digital media championing misogyny, consumerism, egoism, cynicism, and nihilism, all conspire to produce a multiply challenged, if not traumatized, student body with a variety of powerful needs in a failing service economy. Classrooms populated by such alienated, fragmented, multiply challenged students demand an emphasis on slower, deeper, and more reflective and transparent learning designed to capture interest and attention, rekindle motivation, and develop students' self-regulative skills. Contemplative practices are just the right choice.

Consider just one contemplative practice: mindfulness. Mindfulness is the meditative act of paying close, nonjudgmental attention to the features of present-moment experience such as breath, bodily sensation, and thought. It is the antidote to mindlessness—the characteristic of scattered attention and the main problem for most community college students. No matter what the focal point is, focusing the mind collects disbursed mental energy and directs it. As the research reviewed in this chapter will show, the meditative mind cultivates a variety of traits essential to flourishing in community college, including self-regulation, intrinsic curiosity, attentiveness, focus, equanimity, responsiveness, and centeredness.

Differentiating Contemplative Practices, Studies, and Pedagogy

Contemplative practices are exercises in meditative reflection. The field of contemplative studies examines the history, methodology, and theory of contemplative practices. And contemplative pedagogy is the philosophy of education that espouses the academic use of contemplative practices.

Contemplative Practices.   Contemplative practices are metacognitive exercises in which attention is focused on any element of conscious experience. Examples include mindfulness, gazing at an object, studying a single sound, contemplating a word, beholding an image, and freewriting (writing one's stream of consciousness). They are used for stress reduction, self-examination, self-development, creativity, and other similar purposes.

Mindfulness is an exemplar in the scientific and medical research literature because it is the form of meditation most studied since shown effective in initial studies (Shapiro, Brown, and Astin, 2009). One-pointedness goes hand-in-hand with mindfulness and involves focusing attention on one point (often the breath, but any element of experience may serve as its target). Some element of one-pointedness is found in almost all forms of meditation (Goleman, 1988). To grasp its mechanics, consider candle gazing. The technique is to gaze softly at the center of the flame, focus one's visual attention there, and gently refocus there whenever attention wanders. The same technique applies to any target; the practice of repeatedly reorienting a wandering mind trains attention, generates concentration, and increasingly strengthens the ability to concentrate (Rose, 2009–2010).

William James (1918) said that an education that would improve the ability to focus attention *at will* would be ideal. While almost every meditation exercise involves some element of focusing attention, one-pointedness consists in precisely this discipline. Thus, one-pointedness training constitutes ideal education. This is an Archimedean point: since an element of one-pointedness is present in almost every form of meditation, this justification extends to all of them.

One-pointedness and mindfulness practices overlap and enhance each other. Their differences are subtle but may be clarified by comparing the breath flowing in and out to a saw cutting a log. If one focuses on the exact point at which the saw's teeth contact the log, this is analogous to a narrow form of one-pointedness of the breath where it enters and exits the nostrils, whereas mindfulness is paying attention to all the details present at that narrow focal point: to each saw-tooth cutting the log, its sound, vibration, and scent, and likewise to each feature of breathing (Rose, 2009–2010). One-pointedness involves controlling the target scope of attention and training it to one narrow range, such as the zoom lens of a camera, whereas mindfulness is the clear, focused, observing attention within that narrow target scope. By holding the aim and scope of attention on one point, one is better able to be mindful of and examine all that is going on at that point, and by being mindful of all that is going on at one point, one is better able to hold attention on that one point. Practicing either one-pointedness or mindfulness therefore contributes some skill development to the other.

These are representative meditation techniques, and there are many others, but most are variations on these. There are many other kinds of contemplative exercises such as relaxation techniques, visualizations, and writing exercises. A relaxation exercise might involve progressive, systematic tensing and releasing of muscles throughout the body. Visualization might involve imagining what it is like to be the character one is about to role-play, a calm sea, or any other image, entity, process, or state that one wants to simulate. In freewriting, thoughts are written down spontaneously and without editing, thereby loosening the creative floodgates. All of these techniques involve reframing the parameters of conscious experience in some way that fosters brainstorming, going "meta" (metacognitive) by reflecting on the mental process involved while engaged in the activity and expanding one's reference. They are also intrinsically interesting, curiosity-invoking, engaging, and philosophically fun experiences. Community college students overwhelmingly perceive these techniques as refreshing, empowering, and transformative.

Contemplative Pedagogies. Contemplative pedagogies are philosophies of education that promote the use of contemplative practices as valid modes not only of teaching and learning but of knowledge construction and inquiry. Some concrete examples may help illustrate what is meant by contemplative pedagogy. In my discipline, philosophy, many arguments and thought experiments lend themselves to experiential amplification by way of contemplation. For instance, students who are imagining being a prisoner in Plato's cave, living in a *Matrix*-like illusion, or engaging in some philosophical role reversal find that it is enriching to engage such speculations more experientially by envisioning them from within a meditative state.

While topics in philosophy lend themselves to a meditative spin, subjects such as science, technology, engineering, mathematics, accounting, finance, and business management might not so easily. Nevertheless, content-driven contemplative exercises can be generated even in physics, say, about what happens near the speed of light, with time travel, frames of reference, space-time, or the multiverse hypothesis. Michelle Francl, a chemist at Bryn Mawr College, recently presented a Web seminar on contemplative practices in the science classroom (Francl, 2009), and Daniel Barbezat (2009), an economist at Amherst College, has students practice a loving-kindness meditation to test for changes in their self-interest-revealing responses on standard economic surveys and using the (positive) results to spark reflection on utilitarian economic assumptions. Surely any awareness exercise can help students strengthen attention, any breathing exercise can help them de-stress before an exam, and any reflective writing exercise can help them "go meta" regarding their own learning process, regardless of the discipline. These are all valid reasons to consider adopting a contemplative pedagogy.

In her introductory art survey course, Joanna Ziegler typically displays only one or a few slides during a semester, though her peers typically show hundreds (Wadham, 2009). As the class gazes at the same piece for weeks on end, she asks her students repeatedly to describe what they see, as opposed to what they think it means or what they know about the context in which it was created. She disciplines them in the art of differentiating between observational and interpretive elements and postpones examination of interpretive elements and a more integrated analysis to later in the semester. Ziegler claims that this approach develops the basic methodological skills of the seasoned art critic. She acknowledges that the traditionally taught student gains greater informational volume but concludes that the methodological skills are more valuable, empowering, and lasting. B. F. Skinner once said that education is what remains after one has forgotten what one has learned. Here, what methodological skill remains once the details of both kinds of learning have been forgotten is clearly more valuable.

Of course, this invokes debates over traditional depth versus coverage and process versus product, and although students need both (Bransford, 1999), what we clearly have at the community college level is a case of triage in which depth and skill matter more. Intuitively, this pedagogy of methodological skills development cultivates more of an increasingly functional, user-friendly epistemic framework within which to process and construct new knowledge than does the pedagogy of information acquisition, and the development of such skills is more empowering for community college students. The same holds in most areas of knowledge in which an analogue of the meta-level analysis depicted in that single-slide art class is achieved.

Ziegler's technique involves a visual form of mindfulness meditation called *beholding* (Dustin and Ziegler, 2005). Any assignment in any discipline that creates an analogue of beholding of the subject matter ought to yield similar results, even if only for a few minutes, in addition to the time spent discursively engaging the same subject matter. Thus, *lectio divina,* a form of text-based meditation from the monastic tradition that involves reflective dwelling on a short passage, is a textual analogue of visual beholding, so it ought to engender similar results. Beholding a short film clip, equation, argument, assumption, or diagram might support a meta-analysis in which epistemic or ontological, subjective or objective, intrinsic or extrinsic, and other cognitive distinctions (analogous to Ziegler's) are driven home at the level of skill. Most of us have heard of the proverbial professor who all semester basically beholds a single word, concept, assumption, sentence, dilemma, or other intellectual curiosity and how rich that experience was.

Similarly, football players practice mindfulness, visualization, or mantra (repeating a word or phrase over and over) to "get into the zone" or anticipate the challenge before engaging in it (Forbes, 2004), as do chess masters, actors, martial artists, and other professionals (Csikszentmihalyi, 1991). The teaching of these and related activities by zoning in before engaging in them may all be enhanced by engaging in contemplative exercises, so any college course may benefit from such an opening meditation.

Contemplative Studies.   Contemplative studies involve the pursuit of scholarly research about the traditions, epistemology, mechanics, and scientific effectiveness of contemplative practices. Examples include contemplative neuroscience (Begley, 2007) and contemplative historical research, which examines the role of contemplative practices within ancient wisdom traditions (Andressen and Foreman, 2000) or comparatively (Hadot, 1995; Goleman, 1988). Since the focus of this volume is contemplative pedagogy, we will refer only to that segment of contemplative studies that involves research on the relationship between contemplative practices and learning.

Arguments

A calm, clear, focused mind is ideal for both faculty and students. Such a mind is intrinsically philosophical—not in the dialectical or Socratic sense familiar in the West, but in the sense involved with contacting the deeper ground of being within one's own experience, or what may be called the contemplative mood. Putting students in touch with a philosophically vital but nondiscursive dimension of being is intuitively interesting and worthwhile.

Classes that meditate together and engage in other contemplative exercises create safe spaces for opening up that are normally unavailable to the highly stressed, multiply challenged, and generally alienated community college student. Most faculty resistant to or uninterested in innovative pedagogy assume that prepared and motivated students will learn regardless of which pedagogical style an instructor employs and that the unprepared and unmotivated will not learn no matter what pedagogy modulates their educational experience. All indicators seem to suggest, however, that contemplative pedagogies make a real difference, as we shall see shortly.

Professors who set aside time for slow, reflective, contemplative inquiry create spaces for safe, creative exploration unavailable under the informational model. They demonstrate a commitment to depth over coverage, sending an implicit but powerful message to students who have been rushed through mountains of information and whose voices have been neglected for twelve or more years: that they matter. The environmental field and group dynamics that these factors make possible help to sustain not only student-centered learning but motivated teaching. The professor who meditates with students is supporting not only her students but herself against teacher burnout and other ills that threaten motivation on a daily basis.

Objections.   Robert Nozick (1981) objects to the validity of the meditative state. Absent belief in a supramundane reality of the sort posited by the Hindu or Buddhist, the meditative mind is just the brain on idle, so to speak. Applying this to the classroom, one could argue that community college students' brains are already idling too much. Gilbert Ryle (1949) also raised an objection to the notion of introspection: the idea that one can passively observe one's mind without interfering with it is contradictory, for one cannot passively observe oneself in a state of rage—either the rage has to go or the passive observation. Applying this to the classroom, one could argue that the notions of mindfulness and the like are incoherent, the last thing we would want to foist on our students.

Replies.   The majority of the by-now-well-known benefits of meditation are empirically verified independent of supramundane belief systems, and students' minds are better described as suffering from something the opposite of idling, akin to attention-deficit hyperactivity disorder. Rather than idling quietly, ready to learn, they are scattered all over the place and have extremely short attention spans. Attention training is precisely what they need, James would claim, to be able to enter class calm and clear-minded (idling), ready to learn. Contemplative practices provide that training. It is precisely because the meditative element in the mind interferes with the otherwise-scattered mental state that meditation works. Thus, by bringing students into a calm, clear, meditative state, we are able to reduce agitation, confusion, disinterest, and distraction.

Research.   Numerous scientific studies attest to the interest- and attention-enhancing (Lau and others, 2006; Lutz and others, 2008a), stress-reducing (Benson and Stark, 1997), and related cognitive and affective properties of meditation practices (Davidson and others, 2003); that these practices have a positive impact on high school students (Benson and others, 1994), college students (Deckro and others, 2002), and on learning in general (Bransford, 1999); and that they increase neuroplasticity and brain power (Begley, 2007). In addition to the Garrison report on K-12 contemplative pedagogy (2005), a more recent comprehensive review of research on the effects of meditation on learning reports an impressive and pedagogically persuasive variety of positive results regarding cognitive and academic performance measures and general functioning (Shapiro, Brown, and Astin, 2009). This research collectively shows that mindfulness improves the ability to maintain preparedness, orient attention, process information quickly and accurately, handle stress, regulate emotional reactions, and cultivate positive psychological states; that one-pointedness practice improves academic achievement; and that meditation enhances creativity, social skills, and empathetic responses. These findings clearly justify a shift toward contemplative pedagogies.

Regarding the ability to maintain preparedness, for instance, Kasulis (1985) summarizes research on Zen practitioners, indicating their ceaseless responsiveness to repeated stimuli that the ordinary mind normally screens off. Clearly the contemplative mind is anything but dull while idling; it is instead alive to the subtlest nuances of even repetitive experience, a clear virtue for any student. In terms of the relationship between orienting attention and regulating emotion, studies conducted using the Toronto Mindfulness Scale (Lau and others, 2006) show that mindfulness engenders intrinsic interest, heightened attention, and detachment—what Gilbert Ryle thought incompatible with rage. Intrinsically interested, highly attentive, emotionally centered students are ideal students in any college course; they are in great demand in community colleges, where more nontraditional students face greater challenges than traditional ones, such as the pressures of jobs and children.

Studies on the brains of long-term loving kindness meditation practitioners reveal more neural matter and syntactic activity in the empathy centers of the brain attention (Lutz and others, 2008b), and studies on the brains of long-term mindfulness and one-pointedness practitioners reveal similar results regarding the neural circuitry of attention (Lutz and others, 2008a). These results have clear positive implications for both the social-emotional and cognitive dimensions of learning. The proverbial virtues of meditation are not "all in the mind," but also "all in the brain." Contemplative neuroscience is revealing a host of learning-related neuro-plasticities connected with meditative practices (Begley, 2007).

Research on learning reveals that metacognitive activities—activities that loop reflectively back on themselves, such as thinking about thoughts or wanting to have other wants—are essential to the sort of self-regulation that supports ideal learning (Bransford, 1999). Contemplative practices are metacognitive attention-training exercises. It follows logically, and cannot be overemphasized, that research on learning establishes that since meditation is metacognitive training, it supports ideal learning, if not education par excellence, given James's argument for attention training and the fact that meditation is the science of metacognitive attention-training par excellence. Teaching students this skill is akin to teaching the poor how to farm instead of just feeding them.

Finally, some in-class research from my own campus is revealing. Two colleagues running informal experiments in their physics and sociology courses, exposing only one of two otherwise equal course sections to a simple two-minute breath meditation exercise before an exam, claim that students exposed to the meditation before exams scored statistically significantly higher than those in the control groups, indicating a relationship between the centering effects of the practice and cognitive performance. Given that the majority of community college students have a purely instrumental attitude toward learning and a nonphilosophical attitude of epistemic confidence in their own beliefs, effectuating a shift in their attitudes in these two categories constitutes two core teaching and learning objectives in my own philosophy classes. Research on the effects of meditation on my own students shows greater shifts in philosophical attitudes in classes with greater exposure to meditation. One is a shift from an instrumental attitude toward education to one of intrinsic interest; another is a shift from certainty to uncertainty. It is another Archimedean point that my core teaching and learning objectives are better served by meditating with my students than they are solely by my attempts to engage with my students in Socratic dialogue.

Conclusion

The selection of a pedagogical philosophy is and ought to be a matter of individual instructor choice. This chapter has presented the major arguments in support of making that choice. Chapter Two by Maria Lichtmann extends that argument, and subsequent chapters amplify the rationale and applicability of contemplative pedagogy in various disciplines and programs. I end this chapter with an observation from my favorite meditation teacher, Ram Dass, who once said that a key benefit of his lifetime practice of meditation may be seen by its absence during those times he temporarily lost the practice. He said he found himself at those times walking around with a lot of what he referred to as undigested experiences. Our students come to us with twelve or more years of undigested information and about eighteen years of undigested consumerist media programming, if not undigested traumas. They need time to digest and reflect on what they know, what they do not know, and what they need to know. So do most of the rest of us.

Contemplative pedagogy need not involve esoteric practices. Almost any classroom exercise may be transformed into a contemplative one simply by treating it the way Ziegler treats a slide in her art classes: by slowing down the activity long enough to behold—to facilitate deep attention to and intimate familiarity with—the object of study, whether it is a slide, textual passage, equation, claim, or argument. Beginning any class with a simple exercise in mindfulness or pointedness, focused on anything, promises to help sustain an attitude, in both students and faculty, of beholding throughout what follows.

References

Andressen, J., and Forman, R.K.C. *Cognitive Models and Spiritual Maps.* Charlottesville, Va.: Imprint, 2000.

Barbezat, D. "Consumption and the Pursuit of Happiness." Retrieved Apr. 23, 2009, from http://vimeo.com/5224783.

Begley, S. *Train Your Mind, Change Your Brain.* New York: Ballantine, 2007.

Benson, H., and Stark, M. *Timeless Healing: The Power and Biology of Belief.* New York: Simon and Schuster, 1997.

Benson, H., and others. "Increases in Positive Psychological Characteristics with the New Relaxation Response Curriculum in High School Students." *Journal for Research and Development in Education,* 1994, 27, 226–231.

Bransford, J. "Report of the National Research Council's Committee on Developments in the Science of Learning." In J. Bransford, A. Brown, and R. Cocking (eds.), *How People Learn: Brain, Mind, Experience, and School.* Washington, D.C.: National Academies Press, 1999.

Bush, M. "Foreword." *Teachers College Record,* 2006, *108,* 1721–1722.

Csikszentmihalyi, M. *Flow: The Psychology of Optimal Experience.* New York: HarperCollins, 1991.

Davidson, R. J., and others. "Alterations in Brain and Immune Function Produced by Mindfulness Meditation." *Psychosomatic Medicine,* 2003, *65,* 564–570.

Deckro, G., and others. "The Evaluation of a Mind/Body Intervention to Reduce Psychological Distress and Perceived Stress in College Students." *Journal of American College Health,* 2002, *50,* 281-287.

Dustin, C., and Ziegler, J. *Practicing Mortality: Art, Philosophy, and Contemplative Seeing.* New York: Palgrave Macmillan, 2005.

Forbes, D. *Boyz 2 Buddhas: Counseling Urban High School Male Athletes in the Zone.* New York: Peter Lang, 2004.

Francl, M. "Contemplative Practices in the Science Classroom: Practical Approaches to the Impractical / Impractical Approaches to the Practical." Retrieved Oct. 22, 2009, from http://vimeo.com/7223309.

Garrison Institute. *Contemplation and Education: A Survey of Programs Using Contemplative Techniques in K-12 Educational Settings.* Garrison, N.Y.: Garrison Institute, 2005. Retrieved Jan. 2, 2010, from http://www.garrisoninstitute.org/.

Goleman, D. *The Meditative Mind.* New York: Tarcher, 1988.

Hadot, P. *Philosophy as a Way of Life: Spiritual Exercises from Socrates to Foucault.* Oxford: Blackwell, 1995.

James, W. *Principles of Psychology.* New York: Holt, 1918.

Kasulis, T. P. *Zen Action, Zen Person.* Honolulu: University of Hawaii Press, 1985.

Lau, M. A., and others. "The Toronto Mindfulness Scale: Development and Validation." *Journal of Clinical Psychology,* 2006, *62,* 1445–1467.

Lutz, A., and others. "Attention Regulation and Monitoring in Meditation." *Trends in Cognitive Sciences,* 2008a, *12,* 163–169.

Lutz, A., and others. "Regulation of the Neural Circuitry of Emotion by Compassion Meditation: Effects of Meditative Expertise." *PLoS ONE,* 2008b, *3,* 1–10.

Nozick, R. *Philosophical Explanations.* Cambridge, Mass.: Harvard University Press, 1981.

Rose, M., and Coffey, P. "Developing Samadhi: Practicing Concentration." *Insight Newsletter,* Fall–Winter 2009–2010, pp. 1–3.

Ryle, G. *The Concept of Mind.* Chicago: University of Chicago Press, 1949.

Shapiro, S. L., Brown, K. W., and Astin, J. A. "Toward the Integration of Meditation into Higher Education: A Review of Research." Retrieved Oct. 1, 2009, from http://www.contemplativemind.org/programs/academic/MedandHigherEd.pdf.

Wadham, B. "Summer Curriculum Development Session Smith College." Retrieved Oct. 1, 2009, from http://www.contemplativemind.org/programs/academic/08Summer_Session_Report.pdf.

RICK REPETTI *is assistant professor of philosophy at Kingsborough Community College in Brooklyn, New York.*

2

Contemplative teaching can offer both teachers and students a middle way between two reigning fundamentalisms: the secularist one of nonadvocacy, relativism, and equivocation and the forced univocity of fundamentalism. Its antidote is the depth, relatedness, and even transcendence of a contemplative teaching style.

Community College as Liminal Space

Maria R. Lichtmann

The community college stands in a liminal space between world and school and between life experience and academy. With its open access, diversity, and inclusiveness, it is so close to the rawness of experiences that the necessity for a depth of reflection on that experience becomes even more imperative. Although it is an unusually porous institutional venue, it can turn transition into transformation for its students. In the best sense of the word, its purpose is vocational, aimed not only at training but, as Kip Scott describes in Chapter Nine, at teaching for *vocatio*, or calling. But it is difficult to listen for a calling in the din of competing cultural narratives. Teacher and students carry the world into what was once the almost monastic space of the college and is now invaded by the Internet, the iPod, and YouTube. The jobs most students must hold, the lifestyles that tend to pull them away, and the family responsibilities laid on some at too young an age make this a precarious and fragmenting period. Some form of contemplative experience, however we name it, appears especially needed in this threshold experience to slow students down, attune them to their deepest desires, and allow them to become themselves.

Impasse and Education

Wherever we look in the world today, at countries and institutions and relationships, we see impasse. Our educational system is now at an impasse, seeming to encourage more fragmented, less authentic lives in both students and teachers. Students in the community college often appear during

New Directions for Community Colleges, no. 151, Fall 2010 © 2010 Wiley Periodicals, Inc.
Published online in Wiley Online Library (wileyonlinelibrary.com) • DOI: 10.1002/cc.412

times of impasse—the lack of good jobs, entrance into a four-year college, vocational direction—and their impasse mirrors that of the culture today. Given the fragmentation of our culture, with its growing demands on the entire educational system, meeting the need for a more contemplative style of teaching seems a daunting task. Yet any impasse can be either a dead end, with no way out, or an invitation to transformation.

The movement toward spirituality in higher education, and particularly contemplative pedagogy, attempts to navigate through and beyond that impasse. As Belden Lane (1981) explains in an article on spirituality and political commitment:

> In a genuine impasse one's accustomed way of acting and living is brought to a standstill. The left side of the brain, with its usual application of linear, analytical, conventional thinking is ground to a halt. The impasse forces us to start all over again, driving us to contemplation. . . . It forces the right side of the brain into gear, seeking intuitive, symbolic, unconventional answers, so that action can be renewed eventually with greater purpose. (198)

This chapter explores the potential of impasse to be a contemplative space for reflection and transformation and the potential of the community college to turn impasse into invitation.

Spirituality and Higher Education

At least one recent study seeks to address the impasse between cultural fragmentation and education. In 2005, Lindholm, Astin, and Astin published a study for the Higher Education Research Institute (HERI) at UCLA funded by the John Templeton Foundation on the spiritual development of college students and faculty. Their findings, published in the report *Spirituality and the Professoriate,* surveyed over 100,000 undergraduates and over 40,000 faculty at 421 higher education institutions, including two-year colleges. The report raises the question, "What do we know thus far about the spiritual lives of undergraduate students?" and asserts, perhaps surprisingly, that "college students place a premium on their spiritual development and many of them hope—indeed, expect—that the college experience will support them in their spiritual quest" (p. 1). One disturbing finding is that nearly half (45 percent) of the students surveyed were dissatisfied with the way their experiences in college provided "opportunities for religious/spiritual reflection" (p. 1).

The report also raises questions about faculty members' spirituality, such as, "What role do faculty believe spirituality should play in the undergraduate experience?" and "To what extent do faculty view themselves as potential facilitators of students' spiritual/religious development?" (Lindholm, Astin, and Astin, 2005, p. 2). As one might expect, such questions make many faculty nervous about how stable their roles as confident dispensers of information can be and whether they ought to stay uninvolved in students' spiritual and personal development, and I explore this challenge to the movement in this chapter. However, faculty in two-year colleges scored surprisingly high on the spirituality scale—as high as those in Roman Catholic colleges, for example, and significantly higher than those in private or public universities. This striking statistic suggests that the community college, with its cross-section of students from diverse social worlds, is a particularly fertile ground for the development of spiritual practices, including contemplative practice. These scores become even more important when we consider that faculty who scored high on the scale of spirituality tended to score high on measures such as "positive outlook on work and life," "focus on students' personal development," and enhancing students' "civic-minded values" (community service and citizenship)—values highly prized in the community college setting (p. 7).

One of the principal researchers on the HERI report, Alexander W. Astin (2004), argues that "it's difficult to see how most of our contemporary domestic and world problems can ever be resolved without a substantial increase in our individual and collective self-awareness" (p. 34). He cites student surveys that show the goal of a degree in higher education since the 1970s has been making money, replacing the goal of developing a meaningful philosophy of life. The first time I asked a class of students to name their highest value, in an honors course on the great books, no less, they replied that money was indeed the most important goal of their college education, even if it did not make them happy. Although this was nearly twenty years ago, I still remember my dismay. Astin points to the imbalance in attention paid to students' outer development as compared with their inner development, which he describes as the realms of "values and beliefs, emotional maturity, moral development, spirituality, and self-understanding" (p. 36). In most colleges today the focus is on what students do, on tests and assignments, to achieve a high grade point average.

I agree with Astin and believe that the results-driven orientation of institutions of higher education leaves the inner life of students up for grabs to any peers who may have dominance, including video games and rap music, not to mention gangs. Institutions of higher education often seem to collude with the cultural emphasis on external rewards and achievements rather than focus on interior development. Questions of meaning, purpose, and values rarely get asked in many academic institutions today. What is occurring, then, in institutions of higher learning is a fissure between public and private, where the spirituality of both students and faculty is assigned to a private, almost taboo, realm.

The situation is similar with approaches to faculty development, most of which concern themselves with scholarship, teaching evaluations, and service to the institution without regard to the hopes, fears, and frustrations of faculty members (Lindholm, Astin, and Astin, 2005; Astin, 2004). Astin (2004) questions how faculty can find greater renewal, authenticity, and sense of community within this structure. Is it any wonder that despite the efforts of faculty development centers, faculty discontent is growing? A fairly interesting anomaly occurs in the gap between the minority of college faculty (30 percent) who believe that "colleges should be concerned with facilitating students' spiritual development" and the much higher percentage (57 percent) who disagree with the statement that "the spiritual dimension of faculty members' lives has no place in the academy" (Lindholm, Astin, and Astin, 2005 pp. 9–10). This gap constitutes the contemplative space that the spirituality in the academy movement seeks to fill. Many faculty must believe that their own spiritual lives are at stake in the practice of teaching, but they do not need to facilitate that growth for students.

Higher education, then, is caught in a cycle of externalization, of results and outcomes, without much regard to the well-being of either faculty or students. In the rush to cover course material, prepare students for the test, and meet requirements set by accrediting agencies, where and how does anyone's soul get fed? Are educators in the business of the deadening of souls—what Paulo Freire (1989) has called "necrophilia"? These nagging questions come from the voice of the inner teacher, a voice that is never completely stilled even in our moments of greatest success.

Test-driven, harried teaching can be changed to focus, go deeper, and connect to larger and more personal stories. We educators have to learn as much as anyone else the great secret of life that Sister Joan Chittister (2000) articulates:

> The gift of life, the secret of life, is that it must be developed from the inside out, from what we bring to it from within ourselves, not from what we collect or consume as we go through it, not even from what we experience in the course of it. It is not circumstance that makes or destroys a life. Anyone who has survived the death of a lover, the loss of a position, the end of a dream, the enmity of a friend knows that [p. 14].

The secret emerges when we find contemplation in the midst of faculty members' often overly burdened and frantic teaching lives. With larger class sizes and more institutional demands on our time, we probably will not be able to give up objective tests, but these challenges give all the more reason to signal to our students that a world of mystery and wonder lies beyond those scantrons. In our moments of silence and contemplative exercises, we may only be able to point to it, to make way for it, but in doing so, we give students their souls back. Only the depth dimension of a contemplative teaching style uncovers what is real and of value.

But here is the rub: How do we integrate a sound, holistic, integrated notion of the spiritual into institutions committed to the *Lemon* test's nonestablishment of religion? (The Lemon test determines when a law in effect establishes religion.) The distinction without a difference between spirituality and religion could become an impasse precluding any further development of spirituality in education. On the other hand, this impasse could be an opening to new possibilities that yank us out of our *idée fixe* of what education must be.

The Spirit in the Schools

We could begin this process by asking ourselves whether there is any place for the spirit in our life as teachers. Are we among those 57 percent who believe the spiritual dimension of our lives has a place in the academy? Can teaching be a spiritual practice, and if so, how? Although the dualistic distinction between spirituality and religious engagement can seem spurious, Carol Geary Schneiders, president of the American Association of Colleges and Universities, describes the challenge to faculty that the second HERI report poses: "The question now is whether the college curriculum—broadly conceived—goes far enough in engaging students' search for a sense of larger purpose" (Astin and Astin, 2004, p. 23). That is the question the second part of this chapter seeks to address. It may be that practitioners in the field of spirituality have a great deal to teach theoreticians.

Between Heaven and Earth: Learning and Life. The congruence between inner and outer and between what we say and who we are may not be fashionable, involving a serious high-wire act between advocacy that tilts toward proselytizing and objectivism that avoids all commitments. One simply wants to tilt to one side (usually the objectivist) in order not to fall off. Contemplation offers a middle way between the nonadvocacy and equivocation of secularism and the forced univocity of absolutism; both are fundamentalisms, and educators cannot combat fundamentalism with another equally closed fundamentalism. Contemplative teaching, then, does not seek to add one more gimmick or game to the art of teaching, but to develop dimensions of depth, relatedness, and a transcendence that manages to escape our most certain of certainties. In my training for teaching religious studies, I have been taught to remove myself from the subject, to teach objectively, which has created a safe zone for me. Yet I know deep down that this is not a place that touches students' hearts or has the potential to transform lives. I am learning to occupy a space between lecturer and professor, between being someone who merely reads back what others have said (the original meaning of *lecture*) and someone who truly "pro-fesses," that is, stands for something and before something larger than herself. Because it is a space contested by secularists on the one side and fundamentalists on the other, it is tempting not to live between possibilities of depth and transcendence within our subjects and a matter-of-factness that lets no great questions be asked, no sense of mystery emerge.

Contemplation and Teaching. For over a decade, programs and studies linking contemplation and education have been emerging at all levels of education. The Contemplative Studies Initiative at Brown University, the

Center for Contemplative Mind in Society in Northampton, Massachusetts, the Holistic Education project at the University of Toronto (Miller and others, 2005), and workshops and conferences in mindfulness have enabled teachers to integrate contemplative pedagogy into their classroom teaching. A survey of programs using contemplative techniques in K–12 conducted by the Garrison Institute of New York found that training in mindfulness and attention developed emotional balance, academic success, and personal and social awareness (Jha, 2005). Some schools use an implicit contemplative methodology by raising questions such as, "What is going on inside of me and how is it connected to history, other people, and a big story?" (Jha, 2005, p. 28). Some methods are as simple as looking around. Gaston Bachelard's *Poetics of Space* prompted Susan Schiller (2005) to ask participants to contemplate the "greatness" of the place they were in, an ordinary (and therefore drab) classroom. After periods of reverie, meditation, and journaling, the participants found themselves brimming with new ideas and a new relationship to the space. Another program, PassageWorks, based in Boulder, Colorado, provides a curriculum for adolescents that expands on the general model of social and emotional learning by acknowledging the spiritual dimension of human experience. PassageWorks identifies " 'seven gateways' to the soul of students" (Kessler, 2005, p. 103):

- The search for meaning and purpose
- Longing for silence and solitude
- The urge for transcendence
- The hunger for joy and delight
- The creative drive
- The call for initiation by rites of passage
- The yearning for deep connection to self, another person, to nature, to their lineage, or to a higher power

This kind of language—"spiritual dimension of human experience," "soul of students"—is bound to be controversial within the secular context of education. But Rachael Kessler (2005), director of PassageWorks, explains, "After decades of headlines about a 'generation at risk,' the void of spiritual guidance and opportunity in the lives of teenagers is still a rarely noticed factor contributing to the self-destructive and violent behavior plaguing our nation. Drugs, sex, gang violence, and even suicide may be, for some teenagers, both a search for connection, mystery, and meaning and an escape from the pain of not having a genuine source of spiritual fulfillment" (p. 101). These programs for encouraging mindfulness and attention training recognize that learning cannot take place if the student (or teacher) is not present. Presentness is a gift the contemplative teacher gives her students as she comes to practice an ethic of presence.

Colleges are making space for contemplative pedagogy in ordinary classes. Sid Brown (2008a), a teacher at the University of the South, asked students to contemplate a raisin for ten minutes, calling it "cultivating wonder," and remarked that "professors use these techniques to help their students learn to focus their attention, become more self-aware, and find a stronger personal connection with the class material" (p. 16). A. P. Jha (2005), director of the Contemplative Education Department at Naropa University, describes its Buddhist philosophy of education this way: "When we honestly and compassionately manifest who we are, without attachment, we can experience ourselves and our students as ordinary and sacred. Such a genuine meeting of hearts and minds naturally gives rise to effective teaching and learning" (p. 33). These projects help bridge the dualism between the inner world and academic experience.

The Christian Benedictine tradition of *lectio divina*, sacred reading, offers teachers an ancient paradigm of spiritual practices that move beyond reading and reflecting to *oratio*, or receptivity of the heart, and *contemplatio*, or transformation (Lichtmann, 2005). These practices can become attention, "reading" our students and ourselves; reflection, turning our subjects over and over; receptivity, opening the heart to change and compassion; and transformation, enabling new birth. The sacredness of *lectio divina* consists of an attitude with which we approach any text or any encounter with a subject to have it teach us and to be changed by it. *Lectio divina*, then, is the practice of reverence.

The rise of these programs gives us reason to ask: What does contemplative teaching mean to my effectiveness as a teacher and, more important, to my students' learning? Contemplative teaching is focused on learning as deep learning, concerned with the whole person as learner and the possibilities of technology in the classroom, and unafraid to make connections between learning and life. In all these respects, the community college is an ideal environment for contemplative modes of teaching; its students often risk depth of learning and come to college willing to grow as whole persons, bringing their life experience with them.

Deep Learning.   The best teachers are those who recognize that good teaching is focused on learning. Although we teachers do not like to admit it, we often preempt our students' learning by being the sole source of authority in the classroom. Reading the *Bhagavad Gita* again with students this year, I was struck when a student told the class that her reading of it caused her to stop and ask herself about her feelings of anger at her job and made her realize that what it was teaching her was an antidote to anger. That antidote was, she learned, the simple gesture of being present, being freer to open to new things instead of shutting herself down through anger. This student had been engaged in deep learning—a learning that is not aiming at grades or jobs or at anything that you can get out of it. Deep learning is a wisdom of the present moment, which occurs in slow time, the illusion of infinite time, time unconcerned with future goals or past achievement. Contemplative or deep learning is the kind of learning that prevents the duplicity of seeming rather than being.

Teaching the Whole Person.   The real goal of this learning is learning to be oneself. No one says it better than the contemplative monk Thomas Merton (1992): "The purpose of education is to show a person how to define himself authentically and spontaneously in relation to the world—not to impose a prefabricated definition of the world, still less an arbitrary definition of the individual himself" (p. 358).

At the beginning of each semester, I pose this question to students: "Although this course fulfills a requirement, I can make it my own by _____ ." Answers can vary wildly, but I hope I am sending a signal that I would like to see a convergence between institutional demands and students' own needs. I also ask them what their fears about the class are. In a course on the history of Western civilization—a great books course, a composition course, and a survey of Western civilization all rolled into one; in other words, a course with no extra time—I gave five minutes of silence and meditation at the beginning of class one day. This brief assignment, not carried out with any particular finesse on my part, prompted reflective responses from my students who spoke of feeling "peace," "getting a perspective on life," "leaving the usual chaos," "hearing the birds for the first time all semester," "experiencing a sense of oneness with nature," "hearing a running stream that became still," and "feeling safe."

When we invite silence into the learning space, we send a signal that we want our students to reach for their authentic selves, not just to impress us. These are pedagogical moments, as well as invitations to let the inner self speak. I have also found that in employing materials that invite deeper exploration, such as poetry and the sacred literature of world religions, my teaching has been enlivened, and my students have opened up to a more personal connection to the assignments. My own spiritual practice of the past several years has prompted me to notice a loosening and revitalizing of my classes.

Technology and the Classroom: Riding the Beast to Life and Others' Section.   It would seem that any spiritual technology, such as the contemplative practices of silence and meditation, would not work with the emerging computer technologies, but I am not sure this is true. The last two semesters I experimented with having students do short reflections online in response to poetic and spiritual writings. The very nature of the writings they had to respond to pulled them in and opened them up in ways the academic essays I had been assigning did not. At the end of the semester, I asked them to evaluate how effective the reflections had been. The vast majority of students preferred the reflections to the critical essays. They liked reading and responding to something "passionate," to "poetry," to "lovely texts which softened the hard facts," rather than the "strictly informational." Responding to the spiritual dimension of each religion led to student comments on their final exams such as, "We all aren't so different, although we may carry with us different stories and histories; the issue is whether we choose to respect one another's beliefs."

NEW DIRECTIONS FOR COMMUNITY COLLEGES • DOI: 10.1002/cc

Distance learning may seem to represent the very antithesis of a contemplative model of teaching and learning, yet a group of educators where I teach at Appalachian State University has been adopting almost a Second Life approach to teaching which they call, ironically, "presence pedagogy" (Bronack and others, 2008). As the authors describe it, presence pedagogy is a way of teaching and learning that is grounded in social constructivist theory. In it, the concepts of presence, building a true community of practice, and constructing an online environment that fosters collaboration for reflective learning are paramount. Unlike learning communities that might emerge from a particular course taught under more traditional circumstances, students engaged in a P2 learning environment become members of a broader community of practice in which everyone in the community is a potential instructor, peer, expert, and novice—all of whom learn with and from one another. (p. 59)

Connectedness to Life and Others. Contemplative learning teaches us a different relationship to the objects of our concern: not subject-object domination but subject-subject dialogue, where the subject is a true subject with a voice of its own that can open us and teach us. It is not a mute fact, over against us, but stands alongside us as equal, as teacher. When we ask what it is that we are teaching, we can answer that it is not only the content of our courses—this literary work, this mathematical or chemical formula, this social structure—but respect, openness, wonder, appreciation, connectedness, relationship to life itself. Or we teach mastery, control, and dismissiveness. As Brown (2008b) puts it, "In classrooms, students learn all sorts of values. . . . They learn cynicism; they learn hope. So do we" (p. x).

When we teach skepticism and ironic disengagement, we teach a relationship to life, a kind of social and political quietism. The goal of critical thinking, admirable in itself for breaking up old "truths" that stop the flow of thinking, can often be found in mission statements and course syllabi. However, the epistemology of critical thinking, when it becomes an ethic, can turn into a metaphysics of nihilism or a psychology of pessimism. What should be a sharp tool for cutting through illusion in order to lay bare the truth, like a carefully employed butcher knife, hacks the whole animal to pieces. Contemplative teaching teaches on the other side of critical thinking, in a kind of second or knowing naiveté, where affirmation is again possible.

We look at an increasing number of objects in our lifetime: the Internet, blogs, YouTube, magazines, and ads. It is well to be reminded of Thomas Merton's (2003) words written fifty years ago that apply ever more forcefully today:

> The life of the television watcher is a kind of caricature of contemplation. Passivity, uncritical absorption, receptivity, inertia. . . . The contemplative reaches his passivity only after terrific struggle. . . . He is receptive and still only because the stillness he has reached is lucid, spiritual, and full of liberty.

It is the summit of a life of personal and spiritual freedom. The other, the ersatz, is the nadir of intellectual and emotional slavery [p. 126].

With even more distractions today, our attention is easily whisked away toward yet another object that steals it from the last. Anyone who has surfed the Internet knows this constant temptation to look at a second page before finishing the first. Contemplative seeing entails more of a looking in or into and counters the culture's tendency to use up. It involves what the Chinese Taoist Chuang Tzu called "the value of the useless":

> Hui Tzu said to Chuang:
> I have a big tree,
> The kind they call a "stinktree."
> The trunk is so distorted,
> So full of knots,
> No one can get a straight plank
> Out of it. . . .
> Such is your teaching—
> Big and useless.
> Chuang Tzu replied:
> So for your big tree. No use?
> Then plant it in the wasteland
> In emptiness.
> Walk idly around,
> Rest under its shadow;
> No axe or bill prepares its end.
> No one will ever cut it down.
> Useless? You should worry [Merton, 1969, p. 37]!

Contemplative teaching employs the age-old contemplative practices of detachment, unlearning, and clearing the space for receptivity to the new. Meditation is a great teacher. In giving students time for an actual meditation experience, I find it is always welcomed with relief from the relentless pace in the classroom and even yields surprising insights. In one class recently, students commented on one of these meditation times: "I really like the quiet and stillness of this and taking time to not think about anything when usually we are thinking about a hundred things at once"; "I think I heard the sound of my inner self. It was the sound of a million jokes being told." Another noted that there are few opportunities to "enjoy silence"; another that "doing nothing is AMAZING!"; yet another that "in even attempting to let these [thoughts] go I began to find a peace and sense of purity/clarity." During the semester, they continued to refer to the meditation practice to help them understand what the spiritual writers and mystics were saying. Students often say they have taken up a meditative practice outside class.

NEW DIRECTIONS FOR COMMUNITY COLLEGES • DOI: 10.1002/cc

Conclusion

Put simply, teaching always has to steer a middle course between freedom and love. Too much freedom, respecting the necessity for students to choose among alternative perspectives, and there is a sense of relativism that teaches that nothing much matters. But too much "love" and the student can feel manipulated into believing, proselytized. Contemplation of our subjects teaches that freedom is always a freedom to love, and that love must always spring from an inner freedom. A contemplative teaching style, whether it surrounds the subjects we teach with the reverence of silence or the awe of appreciation or simply slows the pace, teaches that something in the core of our being and of being itself matters. A contemplative teaching style means making our teaching "big and useless."

References

Astin, A. W. "Why Spirituality Deserves a Central Place in Liberal Education." Liberal Education, Spring 2004. Retrieved July 19, 2010, from http://www.spirituality.ucla.edu/publications_reports/Liberaleduc_astin.PDF.

Astin, A., and Astin, H. The Spiritual Life of College Students: A National Study of College Students' Search for Meaning and Purpose. Los Angeles: Higher Education Research Institute, 2004.

Bronack, S., and others. "Presence Pedagogy: Teaching and Learning in a 3D Virtual Immersive World." International Journal of Teaching and Learning in Higher Education, 2008, 20(1), 59–69.

Brown, S. "Cultivating Wonder: A Unique Set of Teaching Methods Is Helping Students Bring New Focus to Their Work." Sewanee, Spring 2008a, pp. 15–19.

Brown, S. A Buddhist in the Classroom. Albany: State University of New York Press, 2008b.

Chittister, J. Illuminated Life: Monastic Wisdom for Seekers of Light. Maryknoll, N.Y.: Orbis Books, 2000.

Freire, P. Pedagogy of the Oppressed. New York: Continuum Publishing Company, 1989.

Jha, A. P. "Garrison Institute Report: Contemplation in Education." 2005. Retrieved January 5, 2010, from http://www.garrisoninstitute.org/programs/Mapping_Report.pdfon.

Kessler, R. "Nourishing Adolescents' Spirituality." In J. P. Miller, S. Karsten, and D. Denton (eds.), Holistic Learning and Spirituality in Education: Breaking New Ground. Albany: State University of New York Press, 2005.

Lane, B. "Spirituality and Political Commitment: Notes on a Liberation Theology of Nonviolence." America, 1981, 144, 197–202.

Lichtmann, M. The Teacher's Way: Teaching and the Contemplative Life. Mahwah, N.J.: Paulist Press, 2005.

Lindholm, J. A., Astin, H. S., & Astin, A. W. Spirituality and the Professoriate: A National Study of Faculty Beliefs, Attitudes, and Behaviors. Los Angeles: Higher Education Research Institute, 2005.

Merton, T. The Way of Chuang Tzu. New York: New Directions, 1969.

Merton, T. Thomas Merton: Spiritual Master: The Essential Writings. Lawrence S. Cunnigham (ed.). New York: Paulist Press, 1992.

Merton, T. The Inner Experience. New York: HarperCollins, 2003.

Miller, J. P., and others. *Holistic Learning and Spirituality in Education: Breaking New Ground.* Albany: State University of New York Press, 2005.

Schiller, S. A. "Contemplating Great Things in Soul and Place." In J. P. Miller and others (eds.), *Holistic Learning and Spirituality in Education.* Albany: State University of New York Press, 2005.

MARIA R. LICHTMANN *taught in the department of philosophy and religion at Appalachian State University in Boone, North Carolina. She is the author of* The Teacher's Way: Teaching and the Contemplative Life.

3

Contemplative education, including meditation, mindfulness, lectio divina, and freewriting, regularly practiced in a classroom where a climate of ahimsa and nonjudgment are defining attitudes, can restore wholeness and foster engagement, imagination, and compassion in both instructors and students.

The Classroom Is a *Sangha*: Contemplative Education in the Community College

Robert Haight

Our nation's schools reflect our nation's communities. They mirror the sociological composition, values, economic status, and, all too often, psychoses of communities. Although such an observation appears obvious on its surface, proposals to solve problems in troubled school districts (and the corresponding lack of discussion about the strength of programs in wealthy districts) seem to ignore the simple reality that a school district will be a microcosm of the community in which it is situated.

Governmental officials appear baffled that the most troubled school districts in the country are located in the most disintegrated urban communities. They vow once again to work toward making these students academically successful, but without often acknowledging the challenges of broken families, dangerous streets, chronic unemployment, drug abuse, and a host of other social problems. Understandably schools are often looked to as launching pads to solve the social ills of the nation, but they are hardly enough. As jobs have been exported en masse and those jobs that remain demand more advanced skills, schools are told to solve the nation's social and economic problems by preparing students for the jobs of the future. They are given a long list of requirements handed down from corporate employers through governmental officials and warned to provide evidence of Adequate Yearly Progress according to No Child Left Behind, or face loss of funding or even liquidation of the system. One challenge urban schools face is to keep students from dropping out and provide them

New Directions for Community Colleges, no. 151, Fall 2010 © 2010 Wiley Periodicals, Inc.
Published online in Wiley Online Library (wileyonlinelibrary.com) • DOI: 10.1002/cc.413

with the skills, by the time they graduate, that are necessary for them to succeed in some college environment. Meanwhile, in affluent communities surrounding the urban centers, schools offer Advanced Placement courses that count as college credit, the International Baccalaureate, and preparation in advanced curricula for entrance into the nation's elite colleges and universities. The divisions of wealth and class in society are all too evident from one school system to another.

One result of the shift in education from concerns about student development to job training for urban and rural youth (and suburban youth who do not excel academically in high school) as minions for an invisible corporate and government elite is that it has left students and their teachers in despair. It is not surprising that under this set of values and expectations, high school students' most commonly shared reaction to thoughts of the future is fear. In a *Detroit News* article ("Michigan Students Have Grim View of the Future," Finley, 2009) citing a poll of Michigan high school students, the most common response selected from a list of words describing feelings about life after high school was *fear.* The sense of membership in a community that values its constituents regardless of their performance has dissolved. Students are not the only members of school communities responding to the icy effects of the current educational dynamic. In the *Chronicle of Higher Education,* Thomas H. Benton (2007), a pen name for William Pannapacker, an Associate Professor of English at Hope College, writes in a commentary that he so feared reprisals from dissatisfied students that he kept his address and telephone number secret, installed security measures at his house, bought a guard dog, and purchased a firearm and received training in its use. What is also surprising is that this professor teaches at a small liberal arts college in an affluent community. The effects of depersonalization and the fear of failure and the consequences of win-lose education have permeated even the gated communities of elite higher education.

The community college continues to be much discussed as the place where training workers for "the jobs of the future" will offer salvation to a stagnant economy rife with high unemployment—the place where individuals dislocated from careers will be trained anew, where those who failed to make the grade in Adequate Yearly Progress will be remediated, where those who performed superlatively but without the funds to attend an elite college or university will be educated. Although the majority of community college students enter with the hope of transferring to a four-year institution, the media conversation rarely involves supporting general education for the benefit of students themselves. On a deep level, students are likely aware that their educations are designed for the benefit of other powers, and they arrive at the door of the classroom often wary, overscheduled, stressed out, and afraid, one failure away from dropping out.

If we value our students and our local communities as places of interwoven and interdependent responsibilities and destinies, we should attempt to give students a place where they might learn important and enduring skills that have the potential to return them to wholeness, confidence, and happiness. P. M. Forni (2002) describes the challenges and decisions about what he sees at stake with his students:

> For many years literature was my life. I spent most of my time reading, teaching and writing on Italian fiction and poetry. One day, while lecturing on the *Divine Comedy*, I looked at my students and realized I wanted them to be kind human beings more than I wanted them to know about Dante. I told them if they knew everything about Dante and then they went out and treated an elderly lady on the bus unkindly, I'd feel I had failed them as a teacher [p. 7].

This chapter proposes that a contemplative approach to education has the potential to lessen student anxiety, increase student happiness, and prepare students to build a personal foundation. With training in contemplative practices, students will be better prepared to meet future challenges that cannot be known in the present and will develop skills required to continue learning and growing as conditions continuously change. Contemplative practices can be infused into any course to help build increased attention, concentration, awareness, and compassion toward oneself and others.

Mindfulness Practice

Jon Kabat-Zinn (1994), in his book *Wherever You Go, There You Are: Mindfulness Meditation in Everyday Life,* defines *mindfulness* as "paying attention in a particular way: on purpose, in the present moment, and non-judgmentally" (p. 4). The practice of mindfulness develops two root skills necessary to success: attentiveness and concentration. Students today have grown up immersed in a culture of distraction. From iPods to cell phones, their day is a series of responses to bells and clicks. In addition, students appear to lean always toward the future, thereby sacrificing the present moment with the expectation of a future one. I often find that my students wish to be somewhere other than where they are most of the time, though they would not be quite sure where it is they want to be. They have learned somehow to forsake whatever and wherever they are currently for the dream of some later reward. It is as if the thousands of advertisements they have watched over the years offering something different, something new, had become a running loop in their stream of consciousness. This condition has been encouraged to an extent in traditional education with its emphasis on the future, selecting career paths at early ages, and completing every task for some future reward or out of the fear of some future consequence.

Mindfulness as a practice is the simple activity of bringing students back to what they are doing right now. Although it is simple in its concept, it can be challenging in practice. Thich Nhat Hanh (1999) describes mindfulness with a simple example: "When washing dishes, we know we are washing dishes" (p. 3). To know one is washing dishes, one is aware of the feeling of the water on the skin of the hands, the texture of the soap suds, the sight of the white blossoms floating atop the water, the scent of lemon or lavender. For most people, the activity of washing dishes is not quite so simple. While washing dishes, one thinks about the appointment later in the day, wonders what might be in the refrigerator, worries about a bill that must be paid. Attention wanders all over, from memories to plans, and emotions rise to the surface and then dissipate.

It could be said that the only activity one's attention is not on is the actual activity in which one is engaged. This mental wandering, this continuous state of distraction, occurs not only when we are washing dishes but through almost all daily activities. We arrive in our driveway not quite sure how we got there. Did we stop at the red light at the corner or pass right through it? It seems pretty much accepted today that the distractedness of society in general is greater than it was in years past and is continuing to increase. For students, realizing that everyone shares the wandering attention they experience in their lives to one degree or another is often a revelation. The skill that can be developed in them is returning to what they are doing in the moment over and over again. With practice, students find their wanderings more infrequent and more under their control. They become more aware of the present moment and of the habits of their thought as well.

A second part of Kabat-Zinn's (1994) definition of *mindfulness* is developing an attitude of nonjudgment:

> It doesn't take long in meditation to discover that part of our mind is constantly evaluating our experiences, comparing them with other experiences or holding them up against expectations and standards that we create, often out of fear. Fear that I'm not good enough, fear that bad things will happen, that good things won't last, that other people might hurt me, that I won't get my way, that only I know anything, that I'm the only one who doesn't know anything. We tend to see things through tinted glasses [p. 55].

In the classroom setting, judgment seems a requisite part of critical thinking, learning, and the evaluation of learning. How can an instructor possibly direct a class without judging student performance? Evaluation and judgment in themselves are not the problem. Evaluation is a skill—one that is both important and necessary for students and their instructors. The problem in some classrooms is that evaluation has run amok. It is occurring incessantly, uncontrolled, often interfering with learning. Jack Ridl (2009) writes that once he eliminated grading from his creative writing workshop, he witnessed a transformation in his students from guarded, defensive behavior to openness and a willingness to adopt suggestions and improve their work in response to criticism. To engender an attitude of nonjudgment is not to forgo decisions or evaluations but to refrain from allowing a judgmental stance to prevent one from seeing a complete picture. Just as mindfulness practice brings one back to the present moment without demanding that one never make plans, a nonjudgmental attitude is a course to follow on a journey. The evaluation can occur once the journey is complete and one is resting in the harbor.

Meditation Practice

There is a wide variety of meditation types, but all share the common element of focusing attention on an object. Most often the object of focus is the breath, though any object can be substituted: a burning candle (though perhaps not in a classroom), a flower, a photo, a statue. When students have begun practicing mindfulness in daily activities, they become aware of the distracted state that constitutes most of their days. Sitting and walking meditation provide a structure for a sustained period of time where students can practice returning over and over again to the focus or object of meditation and, by doing so, develop their ability to concentrate. As they become more aware of their habits of thought, their desires for distraction from some stimulus outside themselves, and their feelings of impatience and boredom, they accept these thoughts and feelings as they occur with their developing nonjudgmental attitude. At the beginning of their sessions, many will find it difficult to be still and quiet for more than a few minutes. But after consistent practice, they will be able to hold their attention for longer periods, and their focus will become more acute. They have an increasing awareness of self and increasing awareness of awareness itself. It begins to become clear that students are not just their thoughts and feelings, that what happens in life does not determine their mental or emotional state but how they choose to respond to what happens that determines those states. They begin to understand that searching for satisfaction outside themselves can never more than temporarily satisfy their cravings. If they nonjudgmentally observe their desires forming and dissipating, they begin to realize they need not be controlled by them. The students become empowered. They tap into their own power—quite often a power they did not realize was within them all along.

Although it would be optimal to offer a contemplative curriculum to all students, including formal meditation as a course in itself, the practice of meditation can be infused into any course for limited periods of time and can have a positive impact not only on students' abilities to concentrate and develop awareness but also on the class climate as well. A class sitting together for even five or ten minutes in silence will allow students (and their teachers) to gather themselves. Like a glass of muddy water shaken and then set down, clarity will slowly arise as the roiling ceases, and with that clarity comes a renewed vigor for learning.

NEW DIRECTIONS FOR COMMUNITY COLLEGES • DOI: 10.1002/cc

Lectio Divina Practice

One way education has subtly changed over the years is in its attitudes about the activity of reading. Everyone agrees that reading is an important set of skills; the difference in attitude about reading tends to be in the reasons people might engage in it. In schools today, especially in those that employ corporate-generated curricula, reading is about getting information, delineating the significant from the insignificant, knowing the proper socially prescribed use patterns, and "decoding," "analyzing," and "interpreting." Nowhere will one find such difficult-to-measure responses to reading such as "enjoyment" or "satisfaction" or "enrichment." Yet it seems to me that if students learn to enjoy reading, they will come to do it capably (my essay, "Glencoe 17," in Haight, 1997, elaborates on this idea). This approach runs counter to the prevailing practice of emphasizing skills in the hopes that by developing them in isolation, there will be born a desire to read.

The practice of *lectio divina,* or reflective reading, described by Maria Lichtmann (2005) moves students toward reading as an act of reflection. It values the quality of words over the quantity, the essential value of the language over the utility. In the secular practice of *lectio divina* in the classroom, students might linger over a few sentences by Emerson, Thoreau, Wendell Berry, or Barry Lopez or over a few lines from Whitman, Shakespeare, Wang Wei, or W. S. Merwin. The idea is not to extract meaning from the passage so much as to allow meaning to accumulate with the passage. Like many adult Christians with their Daily Bread passage or Buddhists with their Daily Dharma, or others with their thought-of-the-day calendars, students need the opportunity to linger over a modest number of words that express a deep truth. Often the complexity and depth of ideas bear no relationship to the quantity of words on the page. Students seem always to be grappling with large numbers of pages of reading. I often hear them say they must complete fifty or one hundred pages of reading before the next class. I rarely hear them say they must read something that is dense, complex, or challenging yet brief. They always refer to the quantity.

The practice of reflective reading in a secular classroom asks students to ponder deeply some precisely communicated idea. Passages related to a writer's sense of place, to nature, or to fellow human beings can offer especially rich material for students to consider through the course of a day, a few days, or a week. This time lets students slowly develop their ideas about meaning and the relevance of the words, as opposed to the quick conclusions demanded by a model where students read a passage and answer questions at the end, often used in accordance with the questionable proposition of making each class session a separate entity or independent unit. Reflective reading opposes that artificial dicing of time units and instead spreads through the day and week. Students walk around with a passage, read it over and over through the day, and observe it from numerous perspectives. Like the newly rediscovered joy and meaning of slow food, students can find the richness and enjoyment of slow reading. No tachistoscope is necessary.

One example of this kind of reflective reading comes from the Academy of American Poets, which in 2002 started its Poem in Your Pocket Day program. Based on "Pocket Poem" by Ted Kooser (2005), the idea is that members of a community—students, teachers, staff, anyone and everyone—will find a poem they like, carry it in their pocket all day, take it out to read it from time to time themselves, and share it with others now and then throughout the day—in short, take time for reflective reading one day of the year. As a practice every day or most days of the year, students may find that wisdom is more valuable than mere information in their reading.

Freewriting Practice

Freewriting as a daily classroom practice allows students and their instructor some minutes in which to write without stopping to criticize the correctness or quality of the material. Once completed, the writing is not used in any utilitarian way again. This type of freewriting differs from the way freewriting is described in many composition textbooks: as an invention strategy for writing and as a means of finding out what one has to say about a potential topic. When Peter Elbow (1998) developed his ideas about freewriting many years ago, he did so in part as a way for students to break ingrained habits of stopping to criticize writing at the same time writing is composed:

> The main thing about free writing is that it is non-editing. It is an exercise in bringing together the process of producing words and putting them down on the page. Practiced regularly, it undoes the ingrained habit of editing at the same time you are trying to produce. It will make writing less blocked because words will come more easily [p. 6].

Students who regularly practice freewriting find that language pours forth from them with greater ease, and the production of their writing feels more natural and playful.

There are further benefits to classroom freewriting than simply the development of greater fluency. The classroom atmosphere that is created when a number of students and their instructor write in silence for ten minutes is positive and defining. This is an academic space, an intelligent space, a reflective space, the activity insists. The atmosphere of silent writing encourages students to reflect honestly on their lives. Since they know the writing they create during freewriting time each class session will never be evaluated, never be graded, never be criticized in any way, never even be read by anyone else in the class, they are free to express their deepest convictions, fears, and thoughts, and the articulation of those thoughts and feelings allows that low-level static anxiety to release.

All of my various writing classes begin with around ten minutes of freewriting every class session—enough for me to write slowly one page by hand on a legal pad. When we finish freewriting, we begin the class for the day. The students gain a certain focus and clarity through the time they spend silently writing. The thoughtfulness and silence establish the climate in the room for the remainder of the session, or at least until we do something to change it. Students begin to view their writing as something more than an activity they do to be judged or as something to be handed over to someone else, usually an authority. They begin to see that writing is a powerful tool not only to communicate information to others but also to communicate ideas and feelings to themselves. The act of writing makes students more aware of what they are thinking and feeling, where before there may have been only vague notions and emotions. Freewriting in a journal at the start of class sessions offers an excellent means to infuse a reflective element into any course, regardless of subject matter. It is time well spent.

Metta and *Ahimsa* Practices

Metta is a term that can be defined as loving kindness meditation or compassion meditation. *Ahimsa* relates to the idea of not harming any living thing. Having compassion for oneself and for others and developing an attitude of not harming are highly valued ethics, it seems, yet rarely discussed directly in the classroom, especially after early years of education. Instead, instructors write syllabi with rules that ban harassment, profanity, and hate speech, and entire institutions develop policies and write manuals prohibiting violence. Likely the greatest concern of teachers, parents, and students today is behavior, and that concern has spread to instructors in two-year colleges and four-year colleges and universities.

Although fears for security and possibilities for bad behavior lurk everywhere around schools, it seems that beyond the prohibitions and penalties for abuses, care and concern for oneself and others in the classroom are rarely discussed openly. An attitude prevails that these concerns should be addressed elsewhere—in the home; in the church; if in the schools, then in the earliest grades, long before students show up in a college classroom. Yet by the time students are of traditional college age, their habits of thought about the self and others are highly developed. Self-criticism, hypercompetitiveness, and alienation are patterns firmly in place. It is an elephant in the room in many classes. When in my classes we talk about "being nice" as a fundamental value and an object of study in the class, students immediately seem to perk up as if something odd were happening—and something they wanted to be a part of. When we go so far as to practice guided *metta* meditation, beginning with thoughts of accepting and

NEW DIRECTIONS FOR COMMUNITY COLLEGES • DOI: 10.1002/cc

caring for oneself, moving to thoughts of compassion for those we care about and then to all others, we develop in our classroom a climate of care and softness.

Certainly a cynic could argue that forcing "niceness" is simply an illusion—that resistant students could be playing along superficially, all the while picturing putting bamboo shoots under the teacher's fingernails. However, in my experience of practicing *metta* in the classroom, the result has been increased positive relationships in the class—a more positive climate compared with classes I have seen where even long into the semester, the students and instructor are strangers to one another and the classroom environment is akin to survival. Just a few minutes in a few class sessions to stop for a moment, to look at oneself as if in a mirror and practice the affirmation of accepting oneself as he or she is, can calm and soothe a group and make that group ready to learn, and with openness. In my classes, when we make as part of our work treating ourselves and others with care, respect, and dignity, we see the fruit of our labor immediately in our class interactions with one another, and that visible success makes all our further work appear relevant and possible.

The Classroom as a *Sangha*

A *sangha* is one of the Three Jewels of Buddhism, a term that relates to the community of practitioners. In the Christian tradition, a close synonym would be *the church,* as it refers to the people who participate together in the expression of their faith. Thich Nhat Hanh (2003) broadened the concept of a *sangha* as a community when he explained that "the Supreme Court is a sangha. The Congress is a sangha." He meant that our ideas of community do not have to be limited to church, city, suburb, or town. The idea of building community has faded from prominence, perhaps because the call for community is contrary to the current discussions of the community college as an "engine in creating the workforce" and its role in "preparing workers for the jobs of the future." The prevailing wisdom now appears to be that of separate students being made into separate workers to save the economy from collapse. Living together in harmony and living an examined and satisfied life no longer appear to be concerns for colleges to address. Wendell Berry (1990) wrote, "Community cannot survive under the rule of competition" (p. 135). If we have discarded ideas of community for the value of competing against others for a place in the world economy, an economy of fewer resources, of little or no security, then we must be prepared to provide an education that results in more factionalism and more erosion of localities in favor of a corporatocracy.

Our students yearn for something better. The idea of cooperative small communities in the school holds with it the possibility of a return to values of fairness, compassion, civility, and cooperation. Most of us would describe our hopes for the larger society in this way. If we wish to have a larger society that operates with these values, we need to practice them and instill them in our smallest groups: our families, our offices, and our classrooms. Then we might develop them in the larger spheres of the school, the community, the region, and society as a whole. If we make contemplative practice an integral part of education from kindergarten through college, we may not have to decry the dissolution and decay of civil behavior in our society, and happiness may increase in a population that has moved increasingly toward despair. Our educational journey of these thousand miles begins with this one step.

References

Benton, T. H. "Fearing Our Students." *Chronicle of Higher Education*, Dec. 14, 2007. Retrieved August 1, 2009, from https://chronicle.com/article/Fearing-Our-Students/46622/.

Berry, W. *Economy and Pleasure: What Are People For?* San Francisco: North Point Press, 1990.

Elbow, P. *Writing Without Teachers.* (2nd ed.) New York: Oxford University Press, 1998.

Forni, P. M. *Choosing Civility: The Twenty-Five Rules of Considerate Conduct.* New York: St. Martin's Press, 2002.

Finley, N. "Michigan Students Have Grim View of the Future." *Detroit News*, Jan. 25, 2009, p. C5.

Haight, R. "Glencoe 17." *Teaching English in the Two-Year College*, 1997, 24, 28–34.

Kabat-Zinn, J. *Wherever You Go, There You Are: Mindfulness Meditation in Everyday Life.* New York: Hyperion, 1994.

Kooser, T. *Flying at Night: Poems 1965-85.* Pittsburgh: University of Pittsburgh Press, 2005, p. 56.

Lichtmann, M. *The Teacher's Way: Teaching and the Contemplative Life.* Mahwah, N.J.: Paulist Press, 2005.

Nhat Hanh, T. *The Miracle of Mindfulness.* Boston: Beacon Press, 1999.

Nhat Hanh, T. "Practicing Peace." Loyola University, Chicago, Aug. 22, 2003.

Ridl, J. "Degrading the Grade." Blog post at Ridl.com. 2009.

ROBERT HAIGHT teaches meditation and creative writing at Kalamazoo Valley Community College in Kalamazoo, Michigan.

4

Communication concepts can be viewed as internal and external influences on our behavior that typically have an unconscious impact on us. Mindfulness meditation can help us become more aware of these influences as they occur moment to moment, allowing us to observe our emotional reactions to them and enabling us to break free of habitual patterns of behavior, thus broadening our communicative options in each moment of our lives.

Waking Up to Ourselves: The Use of Mindfulness Meditation and Emotional Intelligence in the Teaching of Communications

Dan Huston

Contemplative practices can transform curricula, classrooms, and students. As community college teachers, we are accustomed to greeting rooms full of students each semester who are there simply because someone told them they have to be. The decision to attend college in general may have been theirs, but the particular courses they take are largely prescribed for them, and they sometimes find themselves signed up for courses they do not think they need. Communications is perhaps one of the best examples of such a course; other than improving at public speaking, which scares most of them to death (and which, if studies are correct, many of them fear even more than that ultimate fate), they see no need to improve in their ability to communicate. After all, haven't they been communicating most of their lives? They already know how to do that, don't they? *Studying communications?* they think. *How boring and useless can you get?*

Unfortunately, the thick, theory-laden textbooks frequently used to teach introductory communications courses often do not do much to dispel students' original perception. The texts often seem dry to students and full of common sense. Like many of my colleagues, I discovered these phenomena early in my teaching career. Fortunately, as a fledgling community college teacher, I also stumbled on mindfulness meditation, and it not

NEW DIRECTIONS FOR COMMUNITY COLLEGES, no. 151, Fall 2010 © 2010 Wiley Periodicals, Inc.
Published online in Wiley Online Library (wileyonlinelibrary.com) • DOI: 10.1002/cc.414

only changed my life but had a profound influence on my curriculum as well. Bringing mindfulness meditation into the teaching of communications transforms the course from what is often considered dry information into a journey of self-exploration and insight. By the end of the term, many of my students find the course has changed their lives, helping them to improve relationships with family, friends, and coworkers; helping them discover and modify unproductive patterns of behavior and self-fulfilling prophecies; and helping them to become better students and happier human beings.

The benefits of using mindfulness meditation in teaching are clear; however, how to do that successfully requires careful study, personal application, and a shift in the classroom culture. The emphasis on gentle acceptance of oneself that is at the heart of these practices, which allow honest, nonjudgmental, accurate observations to take place, combined with a basic belief in each student's ability to make good personal choices, can run counter to what many students (and teachers) at community colleges have experienced in the past. Certainly students who enter my introductory communications class are not expecting to be invited to close their eyes and meditate, but it wakes them up—in more ways than one.

Combining mindfulness meditation with communication theory helps students realize the extent to which human beings operate on autopilot, relying on habitual patterns of behavior when interacting with others, misinterpreting what other people say and do, and imposing their predictions, assumptions, and expectations on themselves and those around them. Waking up to this reality can be a revealing experience that helps students gain self-understanding, participate in life more fully, and let go of confining storylines and habits that often limit their communication, causing them needless disappointment, frustration, or even suffering. Part of this process involves becoming more aware of the emotions they experience in their day-to-day interactions, learning how to accept those emotions and communicate honestly, accurately, and productively as a result. For this reason, emotional intelligence plays a key role in my curriculum as well.

In this chapter, I explain the basic logic of this approach to teaching communications and provide some guidance for beginning to implement these teaching methods.

How Mindfulness Relates to Communication

Mindfulness is multifaceted and hard to pin down in one precise definition. It is fundamentally about being aware and fully present. It involves approaching each moment of our lives as if it has never happened before (clearly the case) and nurturing a clean-slate perspective that researchers Kirk Brown and Richard Ryan (2003) describe as "pre-reflexive" (p. 823). From such a perspective, we observe the events of our life unfold with more clarity and more awareness of the internal and external influences we experience from moment to moment. Studying basic communication theory can provide us with a vocabulary that describes some of these internal and external influences, thus helping us become more aware of them and allowing them to penetrate our consciousness. Those factors include how people conduct conversations and whether they listen effectively, as well as their use of nonverbal behavior and their own inner monologue and self-esteem.

Typically these factors influence us on an unconscious level, and we react to them impulsively and habitually (Motley, 1986a, 1986b, 1990; Wenk-Sormaz, 2005). For instance, someone who has been speaking for a while during a conversation may unconsciously misinterpret her partner's continuous nodding and lack of eye contact as an indication that he is bored with the conversation. Consequently she may suddenly become quiet, puzzling her conversation partner who was, as it turns out, extremely interested in what she had been saying before she abruptly shut down.

Although the communication concepts, skills, and problems we cover in the course might initially seem like common sense, actually observing them in the moments of our lives can be a surprisingly revealing experience. In the example, for instance, if the conversationalist who began to feel as if she is boring her partner recognized that it was her interpretation of his nonverbal behavior that led her to question his degree of interest, she might also realize that her interpretation could be wrong. As a result, she could choose not to shut down and take other measures instead to gauge his interest or behave in ways that would not bring the conversation to an abrupt halt.

Mindfulness meditation helps us observe communication concepts as they occur in our daily lives (such as the nonverbal behavior in the example), notice our interpretation of them, and choose a deliberate response to them rather than automatically falling back on impulsive, habitual patterns of behavior as we are prone to do. It is quite possible, for instance, that the woman in the example often assumes people are not interested in what she is saying and shuts down whenever that kind of self-talk kicks in. That belief could be something she has told herself for years, perhaps due to her self-image, another concept that is typically covered in introductory communications classes.

My approach to mindful communication follows this basic logic:

1. *See the world as a clean slate.* Mindfulness helps us see each moment of our lives as completely new, making us more alert and more aware of internal and external influences.
2. *Notice communication concepts.* The communication concepts themselves are internal and external influences, which mindfulness can help us become aware of, that bear on how we communicate.
3. *Use that awareness to communicate effectively.* Applying one's increased awareness of communication concepts can take on an infinite number

NEW DIRECTIONS FOR COMMUNITY COLLEGES • DOI: 10.1002/cc

of forms, including listening well, expressing oneself honestly and productively, or behaving assertively. The list, however, is as infinite as there are people and the situations they encounter.

Individual Perception Prisms.   Human beings have a natural tendency to filter the world through their own unique perspectives and experiences and assume that what they are seeing is reality. How we interpret the events of our lives is dependent on all of the experiences we have ever had: where we grew up, who our parents are, how our friends have treated us, what books we have read. Yet there is a tendency to assume that our interpretation of the events in our lives is not an interpretation at all; we assume it is just accurate perception, but that assumption can get us into trouble.

Furthermore, human beings are equipped with an ability to form generalizations, often referred to as *schemata,* about their experiences. This ability can be immensely useful. It allows us, for instance, to instantly recognize a staircase when we see one. We do not have to stop and figure out what it is before we make use of it. However, this type of generalization, or *mental guideline* as Trenholm (2005) describes it, also represents a dulled, limited version of what it is we are actually experiencing. We do not, for instance, see all the details of a particular staircase: the peeling rust on the rail, the worn foot mats, the color of the stairs themselves. Although that is not necessarily a problem if your only goal is to get from point A to point B, the tendency to generalize about our experiences just for the sake of getting through them to the next moment of our lives can become habitual in itself, our modus operandi, and we can find ourselves living an entire life made up of hasty, unconscious generalizations about our experiences, the people with whom we interact, and about ourselves as well. Noticing what you say to yourself (your self-talk) as you go through daily activities is a good way to observe how often you impose your predictions and interpretations on the events of your life. Jon Kabat-Zinn, founder of the Center for Mindfulness in Medicine, Health Care, and Society (formerly the Stress Reduction Clinic) at the University of Massachusetts Medical School, explains, "While our thinking colors all our experience, more often than not our thoughts tend to be less than completely accurate. Usually they are merely uninformed private opinions, reactions and prejudices based on limited knowledge and influenced primarily by our past conditioning" (1994, p. 56).

What we say to ourselves is strongly influenced by our individual perspective and the schemas we have formed during our lives. These all influence the emotions we feel during our day-to-day experiences, and our emotions affect the way we communicate. Whether we are quick to snap at someone, grow embarrassed to express how we feel, or are overcome with excitement, our emotions influence what we say, how we say it, or whether we say anything at all.

NEW DIRECTIONS FOR COMMUNITY COLLEGES • DOI: 10.1002/cc

Emotions and the Refractory Period.   Recent research in emotions and neuroscience also sheds some light on how quick we are to interpret the events of our lives on an unconscious level in a way that reinforces our often distorted perception. Paul Ekman (2008) explains that it is not the events of our lives that trigger emotions within us, but the way we appraise those events. For instance, if someone speaks to us in a loud tone, we might interpret this as meaning he is upset with us, and we may consequently become angry. That interpretation happens almost instantaneously. "When an emotion is triggered," Ekman writes, "a set of impulses arise that are translated into thoughts, actions, words, and bodily movement" (p. 68). Consequently we often enter into what he calls a refractory period, when "we cannot perceive anything in the external world that is inconsistent with the emotion we are feeling" (p. 68). For a period of time, we are locked into seeing things only from our perspective—blind, as it were, to any evidence that we may have misinterpreted something, determined to play out the emotions that have been triggered by our interpretations. Ekman's description makes clear the role that emotions can play in the way we communicate, as well as the extent to which it is possible to communicate based on a misunderstanding of the events we are experiencing.

You can see, then, how useful it would be if we were to develop the ability to observe the instant we interpret the events of our lives. Unfortunately such a skill may be available only to the most advanced of yogis. Even the Dali Lama himself, with his extensive meditation experience, doubts he has the ability to observe "those few milliseconds during which automatic appraisal occurs . . . long enough . . . to make a conscious choice to modify or cancel the appraising process" (Ekman, 2003, p. 74). However, it is possible to observe the "impulses to action and words" that are stirred immediately after an appraisal is made and before the refractory period has begun. Furthermore, as Ekman (2008) points out, meditation can be helpful in developing this ability to observe the "spark" (the impulse to react) before being engulfed in the "flame" of reactive emotional behavior.

A recent study suggests that the anterior insula may be the essential part of the brain involved in observing our initial impulse to act once we have interpreted events in our lives (Craig, 2009). Studies have shown that meditation appears to activate this part of the brain and may even make it thicker (increase its gray matter density), just as athletes alter the muscles that are specific to their sport (Hölzel and others, 2008; Lazar and others, 2005). Although most of us cannot observe our initial interpretation of stimuli while that appraisal is occurring because it happens too quickly, it is possible to think back on what just occurred and how we interpreted the situation once we have observed our initial impulse and successfully avoided entering the refractory period. A 2007 study on reappraisal conducted by Sarah Banks and others suggests that the dorsal lateral prefrontal cortex, the dorsal medial prefrontal cortex, the ventromedial prefrontal

NEW DIRECTIONS FOR COMMUNITY COLLEGES • DOI: 10.1002/cc

cortex, and the anterior cingulate cortex are active when people deliberately alter their original interpretation of events. Not assuming that one's initial interpretation of a situation is accurate and being able to consider alternative interpretations can help avoid misunderstandings and improve communication with others. Although mindfulness is not about imposing one's preferred appraisal of events onto one's experiences, various studies suggest that the same parts of the brain are activated during meditation as were during the Banks study (Brefczynski-Lewis and others, 2007; Hölzel and others, 2007; Lutz,Brefczynski-Lewis, Johnstone, and Davidson, 2008), and Eric Garland's recent research suggests a correlation between mindfulness and positive reappraisal (personal communication, December 17, 2009). It is possible, therefore, that these parts of the brain are also involved in the process of mindfully opening one's awareness after noticing the impulse to react (but before giving way to the refractory period) to reveal the interpretation that led to that impulse. In so doing, we effectively open our mind (or at least avoid becoming "narrow-minded") to other information that is available to us. We may even notice that the initial impulse we feel is very familiar, and if we follow its chain reaction, it would lead to a habitual pattern of behavior. With this increased awareness of our reactivity, we are now free to choose not to engage in impulsive, habitual behavior and can instead choose a conscious, informed response to the events we are experiencing.

Many of the communication concepts students study in an introductory communications course (conversation skills, listening skills, nonverbal behavior) operate as stimuli that we unconsciously appraise and to which we habitually react during our daily lives. As we have seen, becoming mindful of these stimuli and the way we are interpreting them allows us to choose how to behave in any given situation. This conscious decision making can be seen as a form of self-regulation, which some researchers describe as an aspect of emotional intelligence (Pearman, 2002; Goleman, Boyatzis, and McKee, 2002). I believe this type of self-regulation involves increased self-awareness and contributes to increased flexibility, resilience, and empathy, all of which are also considered to be forms of emotional intelligence.

The Nuts and Bolts of Teaching Mindful Communication

The basic structure of my class consists of weekly in-class exercises and assignments that introduce students to communication concepts, introduce students to a variety of meditations, and invite students to use the mindfulness they are nurturing through meditation to observe the communication concepts in their lives by completing one "application journal" per week. Application journals are structured 2- to 3-page papers (typed, double-spaced) that provide precise instructions for students to observe communication concepts in their daily lives, reflect on how those concepts affect students' interactions with other people, and explore alternatives to students' habitual patterns of communication. The journal assignments build on one another in a deliberate, natural progression, as do the meditations students practice in and out of class. The following explanations refer to various forms of meditation, all of which I have learned as a result of studying the work of Jon Kabat-Zinn, Pema Chödrön, Chögyam Trungpa, S. N. Goenka, Thich Nhat Hanh, and Joseph Goldstein. What follows is an overly simplified explanation that is meant simply to give readers an idea of how one might structure meditation exercises in conjunction with the content of a communications course. I use the following terms to describe particular types of mediation:

1. *Focused-attention meditation,* which "involves sustaining selective attention moment by moment on a chosen object, such as a subset of localized sensations caused by respiration" (Lutz, Brefczynski-Lewis, Johnstone, and Davidson, 2008, p. 164).
2. *Open presence meditation,* "a clear, open, vast, and alert state of mind, free from mental constructs. It is not actively focused on anything, yet it is not distracted. The mind simply remains at ease, perfectly present in a state of pure awareness" (Ricard, 2006, p. 190).
3. *Loving kindness meditation,* in which "meditators try to generate an all-pervading sense of benevolence, a state in which love and compassion permeate the entire mind" (Ricard, 2006, p. 190).

I have developed a particular sequence of meditations that I find useful in teaching communications. Each meditation has its own particular attributes, which I link to the communication concepts we are studying that week. The meditations also work together to build meditative skills that culminate in open presence meditation, which I believe helps students develop the kind of open awareness that can increase students' conscious observation of communication concepts in particular situations and help them observe how those concepts are influencing the interactions that are taking place. Ultimately, it is that awareness that gives students the freedom to choose what they determine to be the most effective means of communicating at that moment.

Meditation 1.   This introductory meditation is a simple focused-attention meditation that has students focus on their breath as it enters, circulates through, and leaves their bodies. After a minute or two, students are instructed to shift the focus of their attention to sounds. Approximately two minutes later, their first meditation practice is over.

Students often find this brief meditation incredibly relaxing. Relaxation, however, is not the goal of this type of meditation. The goal is simply to be present. Many students also notice that their self-talk constantly distracts them from focusing on breath or sound, and I take this opportunity to point out to them that self-talk is one of the communication concepts we will be studying and that mindfulness meditation is already helping them to observe communication concepts in action.

The application journal associated with this meditation primarily asks students to reflect on how they are feeling about the inclusion of mindfulness meditation in the course, on their communication habits, and on the ways they experience emotions.

Meditations 2 and 3.   These meditations begin with a focused-attention meditation on breath and sound. They tend to be a bit longer than the first meditation and include instructions that invite them to observe thoughts and emotions that might come into their field of awareness. Initially it is helpful to suggest that students allow these thoughts and emotions to be in the background of their awareness, not pushing them away but not fixating on them either. The importance of not pushing thoughts and emotions away cannot be overemphasized. Eventually I invite students to treat their thoughts and emotions the same way they do their breath and sound: to notice them begin to form, feel them penetrate their awareness, and allow them to leave on their own. This is the first step toward open presence meditation, which allows meditators to experience anything that penetrates their awareness without pursuing it, commenting on it, or judging it. People often are surprised to observe that their thoughts and emotions frequently dissolve quite quickly if they do not allow themselves to probe or inspect them.

These meditations correspond with application journals that deal with conversation and listening skills, and they set the groundwork for much of what is to follow since listening skills can include listening to oneself as well as to others. It also includes "listening" to nonverbal behavior and one's own physiological experiences, which leads into the next meditation.

Meditation 4.   This meditation begins by having students do a body scan and corresponds with the application journal for nonverbal behavior. Since students have experience observing their breath by this point, I use that experience as the entrance into experiencing sensations in the body. Then, drawing from mindfulness-based stress-reduction (MBSR) classes, I have students begin at their left big toe and gradually work their way up through their body, noticing any sensations that might be present—pulsing, throbbing, heat, coldness, tingling—or simply being aware of the fact that they are not experiencing any sensations at all.

I couple this meditation with discussions about nonverbal behavior, and we also discuss the fact that people often experience emotions through physical sensations, such as an increased heart rate or shaking hands. Observing and thinking about physical sensations in this way set the foundation for students to understand an important contribution that mindfulness can make to the study of communication. Not only can an increased sensitivity to our physical sensations make it easier to notice the spark

NEW DIRECTIONS FOR COMMUNITY COLLEGES • DOI: 10.1002/cc

before the flame mentioned earlier in this chapter, it can also teach us how to handle difficult emotions in challenging situations. Conveniently, a communications course often supplies just such an experience: public speaking. When students are nervous about giving a speech, which most of them are, they undoubtedly feel physical symptoms of that nervousness. Mindfulness can help them realize that experiencing those physical symptoms is okay and that they do not have to get wrapped up in the self-talk that often accompanies them.

For instance, if someone is giving a speech and notices that his voice is shaking, he might begin to think, *Oh, boy, I'm sure everyone is noticing how nervous I am right now. They probably think I'm a big loser.* As these thoughts continue, he might become increasingly nervous, which can lead to other ineffective speaking qualities, such as increased rate of speech or mumbling. However, with mindfulness training, he can learn to observe his shaking voice and accept it as part of his current reality. He does not have to allow his self-talk to get wrapped up in it. He does not have to fixate on it to the point that his nervousness takes over his entire perception of what is going on in that moment. If he simply accepts his shaking voice as a physiological sensation without piling on "stories" about it, he can remain open to other aspects of that moment that may be present as well: he truly wants to share the content of his speech with his audience, he likes his peers and his teacher, and he has practiced his speech several times and feels knowledgeable about his topic. If he can allow himself to be aware of all of those things, his shaking voice will lose its power. It can remain shaking, and it is no big deal. But chances are, when approached with mindfulness, the shaking will come and go just like the breath, sound, thoughts, and emotions he has experienced during meditation. Without the power of his thoughts and imagination to sustain the shaking, it may simply stop happening altogether.

This quality of mindfulness has many applications when it comes to communication—when having a disagreement with a significant other, when put on the spot during a classroom discussion, anytime the spark before the flame is felt. It is one of the main reasons I believe the emotional intelligence ability of flexibility is a direct result of applying mindfulness to communication theory.

Meditation 5.   If the class has become extremely comfortable with meditation and each other (which often happens when using these teaching methods), I introduce them to loving kindness meditation. This type of meditation is quite different from focused-attention or open presence meditation, however, and some students are not ready for it. Consequently I tread carefully with this one in the classroom. It typically involves repeating phrases to oneself such as, "May I be happy. May I be healthy. May I live in peace," and then offering those phrases to others. At first glance, these instructions may seem to run counter to the focused-attention or open presence meditations, which consist of not manipulating our experiences in the moment, but instead on experiencing whatever thoughts and emotions might be present for us—whether we are feeling happy, healthy, or peaceful, or not. In order to truly observe what we feel in any given moment, however, we need to have nurtured a firm but gentle acknowledgment of whatever it is that comes into our awareness. For instance, once people begin to observe their self-talk, they may realize that they say things to themselves that they do not like, such as, "I'm just dumb. I can't do that." Once people begin to observe what they say and do to others as a result of their self-talk, stories, and interpretation of events in general, they may realize they do not like what they see. Realizations like those can sting, and it is easy to go into denial mode during those moments. To remain present and open to those observations, it is helpful to realize that you can truly accept and love yourself just as you are in that moment. It does not mean you have to like everything you feel, do, or say, but you can still accept and love yourself.

That kind of self-acceptance makes room for change to happen. Here, however, we run into a bit of a paradox. On one hand, mindfulness is not about change or about wishing that things are different from how they are; it is about accepting this moment just as it is. What, then, do we do when we come face to face with aspects of ourselves that we do not like? Fortunately, Kabat-Zinn has a good metaphor for allowing mindful change to occur naturally as a result of our commitment to being fully present. We can approach making changes in the way we communicate in the same way we approach stretching our muscles. When we are stretching our muscles, the goal is to become more flexible; however, the only way to achieve that goal is to be aware of our limits with the stretches we are doing in this moment, with a commitment to living at those limits. If we stretch too far right away, we will hurt ourselves, yet if we do not stretch to our limit, we will never gain any flexibility at all. The same is true when approaching any communication challenges we might face. Perhaps we have noticed that we constantly interrupt others and overexplain ourselves. Chances are that if we suddenly try to stop that behavior altogether, we will stumble, become distracted by our inner monologue, or become overly silent. However, if we decide that the next time we catch ourselves interrupting someone, we will simply apologize and resist the temptation to beat ourselves up so we can listen more attentively, that may be the limit to which we can stretch. Eventually that might become quite easy for us, and we can become acquainted with the new limit that now reveals itself to us when it comes to this communication challenge.

Other Meditations.   At this point in the course, I ask students to write me an anonymous note stating whether they would like to continue with the meditation. Up until this point in the term, I ask students to try it in class and give it a fair chance. However, I never make students meditate. I think it is important that students do not feel this activity is forced on them, that they make a conscious choice whether to participate in it. Typically the result of the anonymous notes is that 90 to 100 percent of my students want to continue meditating. In the twelve years that I have been using meditation in my classes, I have never had a majority of students say they would rather not meditate. If some people express they would prefer not to participate, I simply explain that I will continue with the meditations because that is what the majority has chosen, and I ask those who do not want to take part to find something they can do quietly (reading, sitting and thinking) while the rest of the class is meditating. From then on, we usually do meditations that are a combination of those mentioned above. I improvise the instructions depending on what I perceive to be the needs and interests of the class.

The remaining application journals relate to self-concept and assertive behavior. I believe the meditation and mindfulness practice students have experienced by the time we approach these concepts makes them ready to make full use of the material. They are more ready to observe elements of their self-concept than they were when they first walked through the classroom door. They are better able than they were on the first day of class to observe how they interpret the events of their lives and articulate that in a way that is assertive when it has to be without spilling over into aggressive behavior or without becoming passive (unless, of course, they determine that those responses are the best option in that moment).

Conclusion

The result of these exercises and interactions is often a group of students who have come to understand not only themselves better but others as well. As Kabat-Zinn has pointed out on numerous occasions, meditation brings us more in touch with experiences that all human beings share: impatience, frustration, compassion, peacefulness, distraction, anger, sadness, joy. When mindfulness is taught successfully in the classroom, students embody this realization, treating themselves, each other, and their teacher with respect and interest. As one former student, Jamie, puts it, "Mindful communication has even turned into a sort of game between the students in the class, pointing out backsliding and keeping each other on their toes, while bolstering each other's confidence, knowing that we are all going through this together."

From what my students tell me, they carry their self-respect, keen sense of observation, and compassion with them beyond the walls of our classroom as well. They are more self-aware, more empathetic, more expressive, more productive, and ultimately happier human beings as a result. Often there is a sense of sadness when the class ends, but students recognize their learning has just begun. "I suspect that this is just the beginning of a long and interesting process," writes Jamie, "which will last, like my memories of this class, forever."

NEW DIRECTIONS FOR COMMUNITY COLLEGES • DOI: 10.1002/cc

References

Banks, S. J., and others. "Amygdala-Frontal Connectivity During Emotion Regulation." *Social Cognitive and Affective Neuroscience,* 2007, *2,* 303–312.

Brefczynski-Lewis, J., and others. "Neural Correlates of Attentional Expertise in Long-Term Meditation Practitioners." *PNAS,* 2007, *104,* 11483–11488.

Brown, K. W., and Ryan, R. M. "The Benefits of Being Present: Mindfulness and Its Role in Psychological Well-Being." *Journal of Personality and Social Psychology,* 2003, *84*(4), 822–848.

Craig, A. D. "How Do You Feel—Now? The Anterior Insula and Human Awareness." *Nature Reviews Neuroscience,* 2009, *10,* 59–70.

Ekman, P. *Emotions Revealed: Recognizing Faces and Feelings to Improve Communication and Emotional Life.* New York: Holt, 2003.

Ekman, P. (ed.). *Emotional Awareness: A Conversation Between the Dalai Lama and Paul Ekman.* New York: Times Books, 2008.

Goleman, D., Boyatzis, R. and McKee, A. *Primal Leadership: Learning to Lead with Emotional Intelligence.* Boston: Harvard Business School Press, 2002.

Hölzel, B. K., and others. "Differential Engagement of Anterior Cingulate and Adjacent Medial Frontal Cortex in Adept Meditators and Non-Meditators." *Neuroscience Letters,* 2007, *421,* 16–21.

Hölzel, B. K., and others. "Investigation of Mindfulness Meditation Practitioners with Voxel-Based Morphometry." *Social Cognitive and Affective Neuroscience,* 2008, *3,* 55–61.

Kabat-Zinn, J. *Wherever You Go, There You Are: Mindfulness Meditation in Everyday Life.* New York: Hyperion, 1994.

Lazar, S. W., and others. "Meditation Experience Is Associated with Increased Cortical Thickness." *Neuroreport,* 2005, *16,* 1893–1897.

Lutz, A., Brefczynski-Lewis, J., Johnstone, T., and Davidson, R. J. "Attention Regulation and Monitoring in Meditation." *Trends in Cognitive Sciences,* 2008, *12*(4), 163–169.

Motley, M. T. "Consciousness and Intention in Communication: A Preliminary Model and Methodological Approaches." *Western Journal of Speech Communication,* 1986a, *50,* 3–23.

Motley, M. T. "The Production of Verbal Slips and Double Entendres as Clues to the Efficiency of Normal Speech Production." *Journal of Language and Social Psychology,* 1986b, *4,* 275–293.

Motley, M. T. "On Whether One Can(not) Not Communicate: An Examination via Traditional Communication Postulates." *Western Journal of Speech Communication,* 1990, *54,* 1–20.

Pearman, R. R. *Introduction to Type and Emotional Intelligence.* Palo Alto, Calif.: CPP, 2002.

Ricard, M. *Happiness: A Guide to Developing Life's Most Important Skill.* New York: Little, Brown, 2006.

Trenholm, S. *Thinking Through Communication: An Introduction to the Study of Human Communication.* (4th ed.) Boston: Pearson, 2005.

Wenk-Sormaz, H. "Meditation Can Reduce Habitual Responding." *Advances in Mind-Body Medicine,* 2005, *21*(3/4), 33–49.

DAN HUSTON *is a professor of English and Communications at NHTI, Concord's Community College in Concord, New Hampshire.*

Because learning to meditate shares important qualities with learning to be a better reader and writer—for example, dispassionate noticing, becoming more aware of inner processes, a faith in inner wisdom, effort made with a light touch, the cultivation of a practice through simple, regular doing—practice in mindfulness meditation was used to help incoming community college ESL students become more reflective in their writing and more deliberate in their reading practices.

Being Allowing and Yet Directive: Mindfulness Meditation in the Teaching of Developmental Reading and Writing

Kate Garretson

Kingsborough Community College's Intensive Program English as a Second Language (ESL) learning communities (often called links), created in the mid-1990s, offer a group of incoming ESL students twenty hours a week of instruction and practice in three coordinated courses: a content-area course, a reading and writing course (ESL), and a speech course (Song, 2006). Studying with the same cohort in a block program helps students establish stronger interpersonal and group relationships (Babbitt, 2006). Shared assignments across disciplines make for greater intellectual coherence through a more integrative educational experience—part of general education reform in our college and the nation (Babbitt, 2001; Mlynarczyk and Babbitt, 2002).

In the fall of 2006, faculty members teaching a reading/writing course (eight hours), a speech course (three hours), and a philosophy course (three hours) agreed to share a focus on philosophy that included both Eastern and Western traditions and an exploration of contemplative practices in each of our courses. Using various meditation activities, we wanted to model a philosophical stance—one our students would simultaneously be studying as a tradition in the Introduction to Philosophy course. We also wanted to support students in their work as language learners, in particular as learners of college reading, writing, speaking, and listening. The highlights of this link were a series of philosophical readings unified by

New Directions for Community Colleges, no. 151, Fall 2010 © 2010 Wiley Periodicals, Inc.
Published online in Wiley Online Library (wileyonlinelibrary.com) • DOI: 10.1002/cc.415

their focus on ways of knowing and questions of identity; ESL reading and writing assignments as well as listening activities in speech class that echoed these concerns; and classroom exercises in each of the linked courses that were designed to create greater self-awareness and increased self-regulation: from relaxation exercises to mindfulness meditation, and metacognitive activities such as freewriting and autobiographical writing.

In the high-intermediate ESL reading and writing class, some of our work focused on autobiographical reflection: "Where have you been, and where are you going?" In the first week of class, we worked with an excerpt from a commencement address in which the speaker suggests that our life path emerges out of who we are, much as a film negative slowly gains focus in the developing fluid of the darkroom. Charting a life time line, freewriting about significant moments, and examining doubts and beliefs while reading the play *Doubt* (Shanley, 2005), students were asked to identify values that were important and to reflect on how this current life phase fit into the larger picture of goals, hopes, and aspirations. We read the novels *Siddhartha* (Hesse, 1981) and *Catcher in the Rye* (Salinger, 1991) through its lens. Our interpretive work with the characters dovetailed nicely with the Buddha's four noble truths and the eight-fold path being taught in philosophy. Both Siddhartha and Holden Caulfield reject their fathers' life paths. Why? What sorts of pain is Holden trying to avoid? What is he trying to "hold on" to? In what ways does holding on to pleasure and trying to avoid pain lead to suffering for both Holden and Siddhartha? Why? Does the fact that we live in a world that is always changing have relevance for our lives today? What strategies do we have for dealing with change and flux? Our group of some eighteen immigrant students, people intimately familiar with change, wrote regularly on questions like these.

Going Meta: Language and Learning

Recent psychological research on narrative reflection suggests that the ability to find meaning in difficult life experiences—the ability to reflect—does not just signal a maturation process; as a practice, it is a cause of psychological development (King and Hicks, 2007a, 2007b). Similarly, contemporary Vygotskian sociocultural theory of language acquisition sees language as a powerful tool in human development. When our prelinguistic thoughts and feelings are mediated by language, we can use our ideas in the world with others, negotiate their meaning, and as a result use language to leverage our processes of change and development. Like a map or a blueprint, language can represent an initial understanding and then allow revision and rethinking. In summarizing Vygotsky, Ortega (2009) notes that like all other tools, "language is used to create thought but it also transforms thought and is the source of learning" (p. 217). In ESL class, students used their developing English skills to reflect on life goals and values and wrote reflectively about their experiences as readers and writers.

The pedagogical goal of developing reflective abilities for life and literacy experiences was not just a personal aim or a feature of this particular course. Such abilities are required of ESL students as part of our exit criteria in developmental English in several contexts. At the end of each semester, ESL students assemble a portfolio of their work, showcasing two essays they have written in drafts. Between drafts, students are often asked to write a process piece about what they were thinking about as they revised and what they imagine the next step might be for this paper. I refer to this kind of metacognitive writing as "going meta." Most simply, it involves becoming more skilled at thinking about writing as an often mysterious process and as an object that has been created by an agent with specific goals in mind. For their final portfolio, students also write a reflective piece of writing that shows, as is noted in the reader's response sheet, "that you have thought about yourself as a learner. You have explored in writing such things as: your ways of working, past and present; your progress; difficulties; your experience of writing a particular piece, or of reading a certain book or article; your reactions to the course; ways in which you see yourself changing as a reader, writer, and learner."

As much as we try to emphasize this sort of process thinking, the ability to write reflectively about themselves as readers, writers, and learners is a challenge for most of our second-language students. This is no surprise; researchers of inner speech in the learning of a second language have noted, "Second language users have a difficult time using the new language to mediate their cognitive activity" (Lantolf and Thorne, 2007, p. 212). These same theorists also claim, however, that true second-language learning involves developing just such an increased ability to use the second language for the purpose of self-regulation in learning (Lantolf and Thorne, 2007, p. 219).

Freewriting as a Practice

To support metacognitive abilities in writing, I often ask students to just follow their thoughts and feelings using freewriting, also called reflective writing (Elbow, 1992). "Look back to your experiences this morning in psychology and speech," I say to them. "What stood out for you? What will you take with you? Don't worry about spelling, punctuation, or grammar. Just keep your pen moving. No one will read this piece of writing but you." Students write for ten to fifteen minutes without stopping; when time is up, they reread what they wrote and have the opportunity to ask how to spell a word or better express what they meant.

One of the mysteries of writing is that out of a seeming nothing—an equally blank-seeming page and mind—there is, rather suddenly and mysteriously, "something" when we write (Elbow, 2003). Generally a prerequisite for this alchemy is the gift of silence in which the writer connects with and regulates inner processes, quieting the "monkey mind" and creating the conditions to commit herself to language. In addition to allowing for something to come out of nothing, regular freewriting, theorists have speculated, may well offer students a first step in developing the reflective in their writing (Mlynarczyk, 1998). Perhaps the regular activity of scanning their thoughts and just following the mind, even if students find it initially difficult, will contribute to a gradual change in thinking and enable students to better know their thoughts, become better observers of their inner states, and become more connected to their bodies and minds. "Just do it," I suggest to my students, I hope helpfully. "Be curious about what will happen, what will come up, what you will notice. And while you're doing it, keep a part of your mind separate, observing this process."

I was interested in experimenting with mindfulness meditation in our philosophy link because meditative practice seemed to encompass moves that were very similar to those I was trying to activate using freewriting. Both freewriting and mindfulness meditation involve honing observational skills. In reflective writing, however, syntax takes the role that the breath sometimes has in meditation. Following your thoughts using language means following the meaning-based logic of syntax and associative semantic webs. This focus should be relatively effortless. Given a line of thought, syntax flows, even in a second language.

In freewriting, the search for ideas—invention—is separated from the task of presenting and explaining those thoughts (organizing, revising), allowing an exclusive focus on meaning. There is some evidence that the associatively structured content space of the brain, in which ideas are linked in complex webs, is organized differently from the more linear rhetorical space, where ideas are expressed in sentences and through communicative strategies (Hayes, 2006; Scardamalia and Bereiter, 1985). Thus learning to separate an early brainstorming phase in writing, in which thinking is open to as many connections as possible, from a later developing and shaping phase may lead to greater creativity. Mindfulness meditation, I thought, seems like a useful tool in helping students explore the difference between having a thought and just writing it down and holding back to notice all of what is potentially there.

Both beginning meditators and freewriters are surprised to be told that it is enough to just do it (follow their breath or thought) and that whatever transpires will be right. In both practices, self-acceptance is central. While critical judgment and censoring are suspended, there is a kind of folding in to the core, a quiet focus inward that allows a trust in the doing, a commitment to the process itself to develop. In freewriting, this means strengthening the belief that prelinguistic knowing is robust, if elusive, and will gradually emerge in words if the writer simply opens himself up and allows that process to occur by freewriting regularly. In meditative practices, the belief in the benefit and the change that will come about simply as a result of sitting regularly is similar. In both cases it is a discipline rooted in a simple doing. Provocative work in the creative unconscious suggests that the best way to change thinking is to change behavior first (Wilson, 2002). Both freewriting and meditative practice seem to share that assumption.

Using Mindfulness Meditation to Strengthen Student Understanding of Their Goals in Developmental English

In designing the ESL component of the course, my guiding questions were: If in each of their linked courses (philosophy, ESL, and speech), students sat quietly together on a regular basis, eyes closed, regularly following their breath in silence, and noticing what came up and letting it go, would they develop a better understanding of what it means to write reflectively—following the mind, being attentive yet open? If the similarities were pointed out, would they become mutually reinforcing?

It seemed to me that mindfulness meditation and reflective work in reading and writing shared many of the same challenges and contradictions. In both cases, certain paradoxes and contradictions are a source of productive tension and struggle. Would the experience of these tensions in a nonlinguistic medium, in mindfulness meditation, help clarify some of the more mysterious parts of thinking about reading and writing as linguistic practices? Would understanding the one support a more profound understanding of the other? In the following sections, I describe three major tensions—unsettling pairs—that I believe are central to both practices:

- Being allowing yet being directive—just being, yet doing
- Giving up the self to a process but still taking personal responsibility
- Being present (embodied) but focusing on thought (consciousness)

Being Allowing Yet Being Directive.   Practitioners of mindfulness meditation must balance both pure presence and a kind of striving: being and yet doing. Although self-acceptance forms the core of the mindfulness meditation practice, conscious effort is also involved. As formulated by one practitioner, "We're perfect as we are, and yet there's work to be done. . . . By alternating between active cultivation and effortless awareness, we engage in a delicate dance that balances disciplined intention with simply being" (Das, 2007, p. 53). This call for a balance between being both "directive and allowing" in mindfulness meditation is echoed by Peter Elbow (2003) when he notes that although self-acceptance is key to writing reflectively, "I've too much neglected saying, 'But you still have to try a bit. You don't have to try for quality, but you have to exert some focus of attention. Don't struggle or clench, but still exert some energy and care'" (p. 4).

As in mindfulness meditation, the goal of reflective writing is to both accept the self as fully adequate (perfect!), as its own best authority, and at the same time to strive to deepen and further its grasp on its own insights and truths. Reflective writing, then, shares the balancing act of mindfulness meditation between being and doing, between allowing and directing. Later I suggest that the same is true in reading. Would experiencing the balancing act in one medium help illuminate how it works in the other?

Giving Up the Self to a Process But Taking Personal Responsibility. The emphasis in both disciplines on the giving up of oneself to something else, a higher consciousness or a putative process, is an interesting parallel given the very different aims of these two practices. In both mindfulness meditation and reflective writing, the practitioner is asked in radical terms to abandon business as usual and to trust in the unknown. However, given the emphasis on pure presence, both would seem somewhat paradoxically to promote agency. In mindfulness meditation and in freewriting, you are alone with your practice, and there is no question that it is your own. Students often come to community college as masters of the unreflective genres of school writing—summary, expressing commonly held beliefs—with no expectation that their work will have to emerge from their own perceptions, convictions, and experiences. Throwing students back onto their own resources, in meditative sitting and in writing without stopping, can bring a stronger sense of agency and purpose to the learner.

I also turn to the meditative tradition when I ask my writing students to identify and connect with an intention. I learned about *sankalpa* from my yoga teacher, who often asks her students to "set an intention" for class that day, to inwardly connect with a loving impulse to which the day's work is dedicated. The practice is rooted in the second of the Buddha's Eightfold Path, "right intention," but in a given moment, intention setting is deeply personal, coming out of one's intuitive knowing, a "felt wisdom," and is connected to the impulses we hope to embody and set out in the world (*bodhichitta*). Setting an intention "allows us to align with the deepest part of ourselves," the part connected to the care for all sentient beings and strong impulses of love and compassion (Moffitt, 2003, p. 70).

In ESL class, the intentions I hope to activate are similarly deeply rooted in personal commitments. As in *sankalpa,* they are not finite goals to be reached or concrete New Year's resolution. Much like our deepest ethical self, the felt wisdom of our learning self sometimes gets lost in the competing pressures of just getting through the day in an urban community college to which students commute through a cacophonous city and in which all manner of student life is represented. In creating this space for students to reconnect with their deepest motivations and learner identities, I hope to provide a strong marker for learner intentions: "Think about why you are here. What are your intentions as a college student, as a student of philosophy, a reader, a writer? Can you connect with those parts of yourself and let them guide you in the next two hours of our work together? We'll check in with them again at the end of class." My students have come to the United States to get an education. They deeply want to learn English. They have strong hopes for the future. Reconnecting with those facts on a regular basis, however briefly, seems helpful in supporting these at-risk students to stay the course in a demanding, distracting environment.

Being Present (Embodied) While Focusing on Thought. Regular experiences with mindfulness meditation in ESL class may also help students realize that the inchoate, prelinguistic nature of thinking and the emerging, tentative linguistic versions of these thoughts run through the body. Spending time watching thoughts and experiencing the mind in all its complexity demonstrates that thinking, like composing, is embodied; it comes not just from the mind but from the whole person. Students can be asked to check in with that same space when they write, using Gendlin's (1982) concept of "felt sense." This is how Peter Elbow (2003) expresses it:

> We find ourselves uttering words for some idea or insight or feeling on our mind. Then we pause to attend inward to felt sense—and often we notice that our words don't quite say what we were trying to say. What's important is to welcome that felt sense of mismatch and put attention on it charitably as a nonverbal experience—turning away from words for a few moments. Yet from that nonverbal and in fact bodily experience, we can invite new words—and they usually get us closer to our meaning-intention [p. 12].

Sondra Perl (2004) has worked extensively with the tacit and "embodied" dimension to freewriting and the facilitating of "felt sense." We occasionally used her CD which begins with a body scan, a brief mental visit to every corner of the body, and mindfulness meditation.

Meditating in the classroom involves ritual, and there are ways in which I want also to ritualize reading and writing experiences in my classroom. One way I try to give structure and weight to what we do and to mark it as in some sense sacred is through the use of a meditation chime. After students are ready with pen and paper, feet on the ground to root them in their practice I sound the chime to begin a freewrite. Knowing that the chime will end the writing period, no one needs to worry about the time. It's a beautiful sound, and students have often remarked on how much they like it. I punctuate other activities, such as the request that students read an essay from beginning to end without stopping, with the chime as well.

Why ritualize? I would like students to view reading an essay or writing a response as a special activity, one having its own inner structure, goals, and demands. By and large, my community college students do not read for pleasure in any language. They tell me that they find reading boring. They say they fall asleep. So with the chime, in addition to a more general marking of our work, I want to reset an expectation and prepare students for a new way of experiencing our work. I want to signal that we have a reading practice in college that is perhaps very different from what they experienced in China, Pakistan, or their Brooklyn high school.

Also, as the Zen masters do, I hope the chime calls out to them, "Be present! Stay awake!" As second-language learners, students often find reading a confusing experience. They need to ignore the words they do not know and make sense of the ones they do. College reading for the nonnative speaker is not for the faint of heart. At the very least, it deserves to be punctuated, decorated, and even celebrated.

The bell sound has been described by Arthur Zajonc as a worthy focus for teaching various as pects of the contemplative (Akey, 2006). When I thought about the parts of Zajonc's meditation exercise in which the meditator first focuses on the sound of the bell as it rings, then recalls that sound in meditation, and finally opens her awareness outwards, it struck me that these moves had a kind of metaphoric connection to what we do when we read, and so I also use my chime to illustrate the reading task for my reluctant readers. Zajonc points out that the initial vibrant sound of the bell or chime invites the contemplative inward to a focus on the sound itself, the object. In the concentrative tradition, it calls for dispassionate observation, focused lightly but resolutely on just this one thing (Akey, 2006).

This meditative move into the intense sound of the bell might be seen to mirror the reader's initial attempt to be a scrupulous observer of the voice of the text, the observer on whom nothing is lost. Such a readerly act requires a strong intention to set aside preconceptions and discomfort to simply discern what is. Balancing ease with focus, the reader is both present to the text with all her personal resources (thoughts, feelings) and separate from the text in willed dispassion, still noticing her own reactions.

After the chime has faded, the meditator in Zajonc's exercise is left with its afterimage—a memory of its sound that can be brought back into consciousness. The meditator does so, summoning back the sound, "listening to its inner reverberation, again and again" (Akey, 2006). Similarly, in reading, the reader is left, after the experience of the text, with various impressions that can be summoned again for contemplation. There's a period of "composting" (Elbow, 2003) or settling in which we consider what we experienced in the text.

Finally, the meditator relinquishes a focus on the sound of the bell, and opens her attention very wide. Similarly, in creating a reading—forming an interpretation of a text—the reader, too, moves outward from the text itself to be open to its wider meanings: for herself, for her community, for humanity, for the planet. We need to identify what the parts of the reading mean to us personally and consider the wider implications of these ideas for our lives with others. It is important to be receptive in this phase, to discern and entertain various interpretations and connections that might change our initial reading of the text completely. It is a way "to open up to the unexpected" (Akey, 2006) both in meditation and in reading.

I like to have students work with the chime to experience how they can mold and shift attention, asking them to consider the alternation between intense immersion and distancing that characterizes learning processes more generally (Lester and Onore, 1985). When we learn a language or write a paper, there is always a phase of deep concentration in the unmediated doing of making meaning. However, we then step back to consider from a distance, to analyze, label, and shape. As in the chime mediation, "These parts of outward and inward experience are combined in a kind of rhythm, where one's attention is given to a single object and then opens out, letting go of the sound and letting it back in" (Akey, 2006).

Reading, too, contains similar rhythms, back and forth, from the local to the global, and then from the global to the local. With time, my students come to use the terms *local* and *global* to characterize moves in their writing as well. My hope is that students are helped in understanding their work as readers and writers by these heuristics and these analogies and that our meditative exercises provide an experiential way in to that understanding. In the field, such instruction is sometimes called "learning strategy" work, and there is evidence of the efficacy of making learners more self-aware (Taylor, Stevens, and Asher, 2006).

Engaging students with the interplay between parts and whole, immersion and distancing, and local and global in reading practice seems important in the face of commonly held misconceptions about what we actually do when we read. Students complain that they cannot retain anything, perhaps imagining that good readers remember everything after moving swiftly through a text once (Bartholomae and Petrosky, 1986). Commonsense views of reading conceptualize the reader's job as having something in common with a vacuum cleaner, moving in a linear way across the page, "processing" words like so many crumbs. In light of such mental models, our presentation of reading as an exotic discipline, a mysterious practice, and an activity to be observed and reflected on serves to dispel the idea that coming up with a "reading" is something anyone does without struggle. In yoga we practice poses called *asanas*, some of which are designated as particularly strengthening—the warrior poses. My use of warrior poses what I call "*asanas* of reading," is meant to point to ways to help students experience and struggle with the complexity of their own task of meaning making, using the words of others on a page. The following are some of my *asanas* for warrior readers.

Sometimes we work with paradoxes, using a kind of *koan*, a meditative puzzle, that I ask students to contemplate. Students think about the possible meaning of Heraclites' famous dictum, "You never walk into the same river twice." Students copy the sentence into their notebooks, freewrite about it, compare ideas in small groups, and discuss their ideas as a large group. It helps when students have been studying the pre-Socratic philosophers and have *flux* in mind as a new vocabulary word. Then I ask about how the same might apply to reading the sentence, "You never walk into the same reading twice" or "You never read the same text twice," and we talk about why and how that might also be true. How is the "text" variant different from the "river" original? Does the text change? Soon students seem firm with the idea that perhaps reading the text once changes the text for us when we come to it a second time; perhaps the act of reading even has the power to change the reader, making her experience of the text different.

We then test out these hypotheses in our reading experience. Beginning and ending with a chime, we read a not-too-long text from beginning to end without stopping. After small group talk and some contemplative silence to consolidate and sift, students read the text again, making a note of anything that seems new in this reading. We share what we noticed that had not been particularly salient before and talk about attention and its limits. A day or two later, I ask the group to read the text one more time to see if it is again not the same text in any way. At least a few students are usually persuasive in their claim that a paragraph they had previously just glided over now jumps out at them. For novice readers who imagine that once over lightly is enough, this exercise is enlightening. And even when students do not buy in to the amount of work involved, experiencing the changed text helps all my students better understand the limits of perception and memory. I believe this knowledge is heartening for them as (non)readers who heretofore had blamed themselves rather than their reading practice for their poor comprehension quiz results.

The nonreaders of the community college come to this status for a variety of reasons. Some seem to have genuine, often undiagnosed, language processing problems. Others seem to come from school systems and family cultures that have never asked them to read for pleasure, create an interpretation, or analyze a text. Repetition of the words of the text itself might constitute reading; other times the initial practice, a step up, is exhaustive summarizing without foreground or background. Common strategies are simply additive: this, and this, and this, and this—what Bean (1996) calls a "data dump" (p. 22).

Another "mystery of reading" *asana* designed to disrupt the additive approach to reading is an experience with the interplay of parts and wholes known as the hermeneutic circle. I ask the students, "What would it mean for your reading practice if I told you, 'You can't understand the meaning of the whole text without understanding the individual parts, but you can't understand the individual parts without an understanding of the whole'?" We think on that using freewriting, and it certainly seems dismaying. How is any reading possible? In the future, I will share Maji Drazvi's (2009) "No-Self" tweet: "I took my car apart, piece by piece. I searched every inch of every part, but I couldn't find a car."

To test out the "no parts without a whole, no whole without the parts" hypothesis, students read the text once from beginning to end. They identify what they think is the author's main idea and purpose in writing the text. A second reading serves as a hypothesis test, guided by the question, "Do any of the ideas in this piece of writing seem different now that you have a better understanding of the whole [as a result of having read it through to the end]? Or do you have to revise your hypothesis when you look more closely at the various examples and other points made? Do you find yourself going back and forth between your idea about what the author is driving at and the ways he supports his ideas? Where do you notice shifts occurring as you read? Put an X in the margin next to these moments of interpretive energy." We end the activity with a freewrite about what students now think about their reading process, and I collect their reflections in order to better understand individual takes on this *asana*. As I read them after class I think, *Maybe I can give an assist in the form of a comment on what they have to say.* I thus see dialogue using writing as yet another way in which students can be helped to adjust a stance or perhaps revise an expectation.

Once students become acquainted with the unfamiliar idea of the plasticity of the text we are working on, I feel free to ask them to play with it in ways I also associate with the contemplative. Rendering, an activity I learned at Bard College's Institute for Writing and Thinking, asks students to choose a sentence from the reading that they particularly liked. In this exercise, the text should not be too long or too dry. Ideally, the text asks the reader to synthesize ideas, one that uses metaphors or personal insight. It is a text with some voice. After ESL students have chosen their sentence, they should be given the opportunity to practice reading it out loud to themselves. Then the rendering begins. The rules are simple. Individual students may read their sentence out loud to the group in any order—like popcorn popping, I tell them. They should listen to each other and figure out where their sentence will sound best among the other chosen ones. Then together we create something akin to a piece of music using our sentences. Taking turns, with silences, in loud voices, low voices, high voices, or somber voices, students enact their sentence by reading it out loud. I jump in with my favorite to create a kind of chorus occasionally. And when the group runs out of steam, we stop.

This playful approach to the summarizing of main ideas usually touches on the high points of the reading. It allows repeated experiencing of those high points in a student-generated medium. The students have slipped in to the text as a group, wearing its sentences as a kind of sound garment. As we read, the text surrounds us. And the reading aloud grounds the text, giving it a more embodied quality than it had when it was just read silently. Suddenly it has substance, texture, and presence.

Instead of asking students to choose a sentence that they like, I sometimes ask them to attend to the voice of the author. Where do they sense energy in this text? Where is the author closest to his own feelings and purpose in writing this text? As they read, students should look for those sentences and draw a heart in the margin next to them. After we finish reading, we compare the chosen passages. Do they indeed lead into the heart of the matter? Usually they do. And I hope students come to understand that they know these things using their hearts, their linguistic intuition. This knowledge is available to them at a preconscious level, even when they do not understand every word, as a matter of cultivating a certain kind of listening. What unifies these approaches to reading is their tendency to make the act of reading an event, that is, an experience or a practice, rather than a simple apprehension of an external object (the text). They encourage weakened boundaries between reader and text, between emotions and cognition, and between being and doing. Such a practice presents reading as a transaction in which the reader, and the act of reading itself, is as important as the author's intent, the structure of the text, or some putative main idea.

A large part of contemplative work with reading should include helping students understand this transactional nature of the process of arriving at an understanding, to which they must bring the entire range of their perceptual faculties and inner wisdom (Rosenblatt, 1995). As in mindfulness meditation, the stance of the reader must be active and awake. Attending to one's own consciousness in the act of reading means being profoundly open to new experience, as in attending to the bell and its afterlife. At the same time, the reader must attend to the patterns of his own imaginative breath—the active movement of his associations, feelings, sensations, ideas, and attitudes in response to the text:

> Linking the signs on the page to the word is not enough. It requires linking the word with what it points to in the human or natural world. This involves awareness of the sensations it symbolizes, the systems or categories into which it fits, the complex of experiences out of which it springs, the modes of feeling or practical situation with which it is associated, the actions it may imply. . . . Moreover, we must relate it to our own experience so that it may become part of our working equipment. Only then, as we place it in its relation to other sensations, ideas, attitudes, and patterns, all equally realized, shall we be in a position to say that we understand it [Rosenblatt, 1995, p. 106].

Above all, text must be conceived of as an experience (Rosenblatt, 1964). Experiences occur to a sentient being in time, with varying levels of conscious awareness, some of which can be brought to greater consciousness. Working with contemplative practices in the reading and writing classroom helps emphasize those underlying dimensions, often all too easily forgotten in the "read pages 1 to 15 for Monday" rituals of our daily lives.

Conclusion

I wish I could claim that these practices all worked like a charm and that adding mindfulness meditation to our learning community pedagogy made all the difference in student outcomes. That was not the case. Language education in reading and writing (and second-language acquisition more generally) probably cannot be hurried, and our twelve-week semester is short. My purpose in this chapter is to outline ways that mindfulness meditation might be used in ESL classrooms to amplify aspects of reading and writing practice that are not addressed in more traditional formalistic or skills-based instructional methods. I have claimed that the habits of mind of the contemplative—noticing; becoming more aware of inner processes; personal grounding with faith in inner wisdom; effort made with a light touch; the cultivation of a practice through simple, regular doing and deliberate focus—might be used to help students understand reading as an experiential process and develop stronger reflective abilities when they write. However, as is true in both practices, the proof is in the doing.

References

Akey, J. "Report on the 2006 Academic Summer Session on Contemplative Curriculum." Amherst, Mass.: Center for Contemplative Mind in Society, 2006. Retrieved July 13, 2010, from http://www.contemplativemind.org/programs/academic/_reports. html.

Babbitt, M. "Making Writing Count in an ESL Learning Community." In I. Leki (ed.), *Academic Writing Programs*. Alexandria, Va.: TESOL, 2001.

Babbitt, M. "Strength in Community: Effectiveness of Community in Building College Success." In M. Spaventa (ed.), *Pedagogy, Programs, Curricula and Assessment*. Alexandria, Va.: TESOL, 2006.

Bartholomae, D., and Petrosky, T. *Facts, Artifacts, and Counterfacts: Theory and Method for a Reading and Writing Course*. Portsmouth, N.H.: Boynton/Cook, 1986.

Bean, J. C. *Engaging Ideas: The Professor's Guide to Integrating Writing, Critical Thinking, and Active Learning in the Classroom*. San Francisco: Jossey-Bass, 1996.

Das, L. S. "The Heart of Buddhist Meditation." *Tricycle*, 2007, 17(2), 50–53.

Drazvi, M. "No-Self." *Tricycle Magazine*. Accessed July 20, 2009, at http://twitter.com/tricyclemag/status/2745878942.

Elbow, P. "Freewriting and the Problem of Wheat and Tares." In J. Moxley (ed.), *Writing and Publishing for Academic Authors*. Lanham, Md.: University Press of America, 1992.

Elbow, P. "Three Mysteries at the Heart of Writing." In L. Z. Bloom, D. A. Daiker, and E. M. White (eds.), *Composition Studies in the New Millennium: Rereading the Past, Rewriting the Future*. Carbondale: Southern Illinois University Press, 2003.

Gendlin, E. T. *Focusing*. New York: Bantam, 1982.

Hayes, J. R. "New Directions in Writing Theory." In C. A. MacArthur, S. Graham, and J. Fitzgerald (eds.), *Handbook of Writing Research*. New York: Guilford Press, 2006.

Hesse, H. *Siddhartha*. New York: Bantam, 1981.

King, L. A., and Hicks, J. A. "Lost and Found Possible Selves: Goals, Development, and Well-Being." In Marsha Rossiter (ed.), *Possible Selves and Adult Learning*. New Directions for Adult and Continuing Education, no. 114. San Francisco: Jossey-Bass, 2007a.

King, L. A., and Hicks, J. A. "Whatever Happened to 'What Might Have Been'? Regrets, Happiness, and Maturity." *American Psychologist*, 2007b, 62(7), 625-636.

Lantolf, J. P., and Thorne, S. L. "Sociocultural Theory and Second Language Learning." In B. VanPatten and J. Williams (eds.), *Theories in Second Language Acquisition: An Introduction*. Mahwah, N.J.: Erlbaum, 2007.

Lester, N., and Onore, C. "Immersion and Distancing: The Ins and Outs of Inservice Education." *English Education*, 1985, 17(1), 7–13.

Mlynarczyk, R. *Conversations of the Mind. The Uses of Journal Writing for Second-Language Learners.* Mahwah, N.J.: Erlbaum, 1998.

Mlynarczyk, R., and Babbitt, M. "The Power of Academic Learning Communities." *Journal of Basic Writing,* 2002, *21*(1), 71–89.

Moffitt, P. "The Heart's Intention." *Yoga Journal,* Oct.–Nov. 2003, pp. 67–70.

Ortega, L. *Understanding Second Language Acquisition.* London: Hodder Education, 2009.

Perl, S. *Felt Sense: Writing with the Body.* Portsmouth, N.H.: Boynton/Cook, 2004.

Rosenblatt, L. M. "The Poem as Event." *College English,* 1964, *26*(2), 123–128

Rosenblatt, L. M. *Literature as Exploration.* (5th ed.) New York: MLA, 1995.

Salinger, J. D. *The Catcher in the Rye.* New York: Little, Brown, 1991.

Scardamalia, M., and Bereiter, C. "Fostering the Development of Self-Regulation in Children's Knowledge Processing." In S. F. Chipman, J. W. Segal, and R. Glaser (eds.), *Thinking and Learning Skills.* Mahwah, N.J.: Erlbaum, 1985.

Shanley, J. P. *Doubt: A Parable.* New York: Theatre Communications Group, 2005.

Song, B. "Content-Based ESL Instruction: Long Term Effects and Outcomes." *English for Specific Purposes,* 2006, *25,* 420–437.

Taylor, A., Stevens, J. R., and Asher, J. W. "The Effects of Explicit Reading Strategy Training on L2 Reading." In J. M. Norris and L. Ortega (eds.), *Synthesizing Research on Language Learning and Teaching.* Philadelphia: John Benjamins, 2006.

Wilson, T. D. *Strangers to Ourselves: Discovering the Adaptive Unconscious.* Cambridge, Mass.: Harvard University Press, 2002.

KATE GARRETSON *is associate professor of English at Kingsborough Community College in Brooklyn, New York, part of the City University of New York.*

This chapter describes ways in which contemplative practices are used in a human services education program to help students integrate self-care into their lives.

Contemplative Practices in Human Services Education

Jacqueline M. Griswold

As a human services educator and practitioner, I have experienced the stress that often leads to burnout in my own life, and I have observed it in my colleagues and students as well. I am often reminded of the importance of self-care and of taking time to recharge my batteries. As a human services practitioner and educator, I believe that burnout is one of the biggest issues I see in this field. Human services work is often emotionally and physically draining because of the nature of the field. Whether one works with victims of domestic violence, formerly incarcerated individuals, individuals with mental illness, addiction, or survivors of catastrophic events, the work involves dealing with individuals in crisis. Burnout comes from being overworked and underpaid, and most important, not practicing self-care. A literature review, coupled with my own experiences in the human services field, supports the notion that individuals working in the helping professions are at high risk for job burnout. Students in human services programs are often concerned with others and their problems, are already stretched thin with commitments to others, are in touch with human suffering, and quite often lack the skills to care for themselves.

The human services philosophy views the individual from a holistic, integrated perspective. In order to better serve the individuals with whom we work in the helping professions and teach them self-care skills, we first need to develop those skills in ourselves. As human services professionals, we believe in caring for the whole person, body, mind, and spirit. We also

NEW DIRECTIONS FOR COMMUNITY COLLEGES, no. 151, Fall 2010 © 2010 Wiley Periodicals, Inc.
Published online in Wiley Online Library (wileyonlinelibrary.com) • DOI: 10.1002/cc.416

believe that one foundation of human services is personal wellness, and a primary function of human services professionals is to serve as guides and teachers. Wellness is much more than the absence of illness; rather, it is a commitment to self-care in all planes of existence—physical, mental, and spiritual. We encourage people to take responsibility for their own lives through self-awareness, healthy lifestyles, and self-care activities. In order to be effective in teaching these skills to others, students should incorporate self-care into their own lives.

This chapter explores the correlation between human services practice and stress and examines the use of contemplative practices in the classroom as a way to teach self-care. The chapter also discusses ways in which contemplative practices can be incorporated as a critical component of human services education. Examples include stillness practices such as centering, sitting meditation, and silence, as well as relational practices such as deep listening, sharing experiences, and engaging in critical thinking through reflective journaling.

Literature Review

Although the literature search produced few resources specific to general human services work, an overarching theme is that stress is an inherent part of the work, and in extreme cases it can result in a set of negative symptoms we have come to know as burnout. Burnout occurs not only in experienced human services professionals but can occur with novice practitioners at the beginnings of their careers (Azar, 2000). "The very act of being compassionate and empathic extracts a cost under most circumstances. In our effort to view the world from the perspective of the suffering we suffer" (Figley, 2002, p. 1434). According to Seward (2008), "Stress is the equal-opportunity destroyer. It affects everyone: rich and poor, young and old, male and female. Stress is part of everyone's lives. Any change, positive or negative, is stressful because we need to adapt to the change" (p. ix). Hans Selye noted in 1956 that a certain amount of stress can be challenging and useful, but chronic or excessive stress makes the body less able to adapt and cope, resulting in what he called distress.

Human services professionals are no different. While noting her own assumption that people who work in the human services are "only human," Bernstein (1999, p. 138) mentions some common myths about human services workers, including that they are professionals who are above reproach, they are miracle workers, they remain calm at all times, and they know all of the answers.

The reality, of course, is that human services workers are not perfect or superhuman. Unfortunately many human services students and workers try to live up to these standards, and in doing so they increase the stressors in their lives, which may ultimately lead to stress-related illnesses and burnout. "Burnout is not something that happens to you all of a sudden;

rather it results from an insidious form of self-neglect, a kind of slow deterioration that eventually rusts and corrodes the edges of your compassion and caring" (Kottler and Zehm, 2000, p. 82).

According to Dass and Gorman (1994), "The experience of burnout has a particular kind of poignance. Having started out to help others, we're somehow getting wounded ourselves. What we had in mind was expressing compassion. Instead, what we seem to be adding to the universe is more suffering—our own—while we're supposedly helping" (pp. 185–186).

Background

Several years ago, I was involved in a scholarship of teaching and learning (SoTL) faculty development program. Each faculty member proposed a research project and integrated the results of her research in her teaching practices. I was also a participant in the Center for Contemplative Mind in Society's summer curriculum development session, which allowed me to develop ways of integrating contemplative practices into classroom practices.

My observation from teaching in human services programs for over thirty years is that learning self-care strategies is critical to success and longevity in the helping professions. Students who do not learn to care for themselves often end up feeling overwhelmed and begin to exhibit symptoms of burnout. Furthermore, from a teaching-learning perspective, the teacher's ability to model self-care is a critical component of the learning process.

Throughout the associate degree program in human services at my community college, the topics of wellness and self-care are discussed frequently. Some faculty members choose to do a centering activity at the beginning of every class, and others talk about their experiences with professional burnout and their own self-care plans. Prior to the SoTL project, however, no specific course intentionally addressed wellness practices and self-care as a major component. Since one of the primary concerns in the helping professions is staff turnover related to burnout, I chose to research and integrate wellness practices and self-care into a course, Introduction to Practicum. This course is designed to give students further opportunities to explore human services as a profession, learn more about existing community resources, learn strategies for self-care to mitigate the stress inherent in the helping professions, and develop a career and professional development plan.

The theme of wellness and self-care is woven into the fabric of Introduction to Practicum and continues to be a theme in subsequent courses. Students are taught specific contemplative practices and begin to incorporate the practices into their own lives. Some students are initially uncomfortable with some of the contemplative practices, but most come to find value in them. They begin to look forward to and expect a chance to center at the start of a class and remind me if I forget.

One model that has been useful to me is the tree of contemplative practices (Figure 6.1), which was developed by the Center for Contemplative

Figure 6.1. Tree of Contemplative Practices

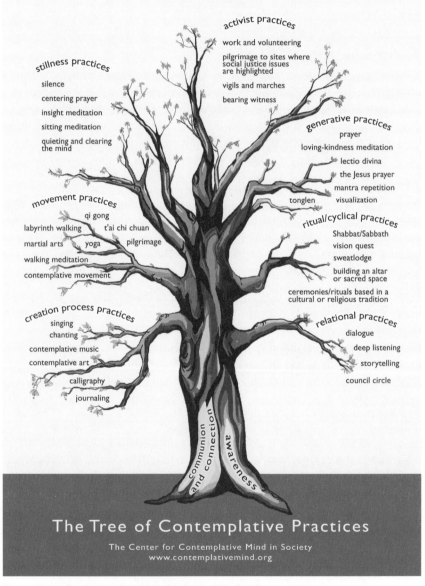

Source: Center for Contemplative Mind in Society. Used with permission.

NEW DIRECTIONS FOR COMMUNITY COLLEGES • DOI: 10.1002/cc

Mind in Society. The tree offers a symbolic representation of many contemplative practices. According to the center,

> The roots symbolize the two intentions that are the foundation of all contemplative practices: cultivating awareness and developing a stronger connection to God, the divine, or inner wisdom. The roots of the tree encompass and transcend differences in the religious traditions from which many of the practices originated, and allow room for the inclusion of new practices that are being created in secular contexts. . . . The branches represent the different groupings of practices. For example, *Stillness Practices* focus on quieting the mind and body in order to develop calmness and focus. *Generative Practices* come in many different forms (i.e. prayers, visualizations, chanting) but share the common intent of generating thoughts and feelings of devotion and compassion, rather than calming and quieting the mind. These classifications are not definitive. For example, mantra repetition may be considered a Stillness Practice rather than a Generative one [Center for Contemplative Mind in Society, 2002].

Teaching Practices

Using this tree as a starting point for teaching contemplative practices, I talk about the importance of building relationships as helpers and the need to be centered and fully present in order to develop an effective helping relationship. Dass and Gorman (1994) note that "much of our capacity to help another person depends upon our state of mind. Sometimes our minds are so scattered, confused, depressed, or agitated, we can hardly get out of bed. At other times we're clear, alert, and receptive; we feel ready, even eager, to respond generously to the needs of others" (p. 93). Bewley (2004) states, "The first step in establishing a helping relationship is preparing to be with someone. We need to pause and clear the thoughts, feelings and distractions that can get in the way of our being fully present with another person. This process is called *centering*" (p. 13). If we do not take the time to center, Bewley continues, we may be distracted, compromise the quality of our interactions with coworkers, or reduce our ability to help others. However, "when we are centered, we are able to pay attention to others and respond in ways that build a good helping relationship" (p. 13).

The following sections describe several of the contemplative practices I use with students.

Stillness Practices.   The goal of stillness practices is to quiet the mind and allow one to focus on the task at hand. They can be used at any time, and are particularly helpful when someone is distracted and needs to regain focus. For instance I use centering to help students with the transition from one class to another.

Centering.   Centering uses breathing to quiet and clear the mind. I teach several centering practices to the students in my classes, and we practice them on a regular basis, typically at the beginning of each class. I begin with fairly short, focused breathing exercises, having the students pay attention to their breathing without trying to modify the pattern. During the course of the exercise, I remind students to let go of distracting thoughts and continue to focus on the breathing. The first few times we do this, it might be for only two or three minutes, and we gradually work up to about ten minutes.

Sitting Meditation. The centering exercise is an introduction to sitting meditation. Like centering, sitting meditation begins by observing the breath as it goes in and out. Our full attention is given to the sensation of the breath as it comes in and goes out. We notice when our mind wanders and bring our attention back to our breathing. "Each time you become aware of this while you are sitting, you gently bring your attention back to your belly and back to your breathing, no matter what carried it away. If it moves off the breath a hundred times, then you just calmly bring it back a hundred times, as soon as you are aware of not being in the breath" (Kabat-Zinn, 2005, p. 65). Once students have become fairly comfortable with short centering activities, we begin to move to sitting meditation, gradually increasing the time spent as students become more accustomed to the practice.

Guided Visualization. Among the stillness practices I use is guided visualization, generally making it up as I go along. One guided visualization I do with students, usually around the middle of the semester when they may be feeling a great deal of stress, focuses on imagining the success of completing the semester:

> Sit comfortably with your feet on the floor, your eyes closed. Breathe in to the count of eight, hold it for four, and then slowly let your breath out to the count of eight. Continue to pay attention to your breathing. If thoughts come into your mind, notice them and let them go.
>
> Imagine that it's the end of the semester. The papers are all written, final exams are over, you have gotten your grades, and you are happy with the results. Imagine that you are sitting outside in the warm sunshine. Imagine how relaxed your body feels; notice that the tension is gone from your shoulders and neck . . . notice that your breathing is slow and steady; notice that all the worries and stress are gone from your mind. Continue to quietly pay attention to your breathing and the sense of calm in your body. Feel the warmth of the sun and the gentle breeze . . . feel the calm that comes over your body as all your cares melt away in the sunshine . . . continue to notice your breathing and enjoy the relaxed feeling in your body: . . . in . . . out . . . in . . . out . . . When you're ready, open your eyes, and come back.

Body Scan Meditation and Progressive Relaxation. In his book *Full Catastrophe Living* (2005), Jon Kabat-Zinn describes a body scan meditation that helps individuals reconnect with their body. According to

Kabat-Zinn, "The idea in scanning your body is to actually *feel* each region you focus on and linger there with your mind right *on* it or *in* it. . . . If you imagine that the tension in your body and the feelings of fatigue associated with it are *flowing out* on each outbreath and that, on each inbreath, you are breathing in energy, vitality and relaxation" (pp. 77–78.)

In my classes, I adapt the body scan, making it shorter, and having the students sitting in their chairs rather than lying down. Depending on time, I might start at the fingertips and work my way up the arms; the shoulders, back, and neck; and up to the face and head. As we move through the areas, I continue to guide the students to breathe in and breathe out, paying attention to the body in each region. When time permits in class I do a full body scan, beginning at the toes of the left foot and gradually working my way up the legs, torso, arms, and head.

Touchstone Meditation.   This meditation has proven to be a favorite of many students. Throughout the year, I gather small, flat, smooth stones as I wander the beaches of Cape Cod in Massachusetts or of Newport, Rhode Island. I bring a box of stones to the classroom and ask students to choose a stone mindfully, looking at them and deciding which one "belongs" to them. Picking out the stone becomes a meditation of sorts, because students choose them carefully.

Once everyone has a stone, I ask them to spend some time becoming familiar with it, noting color, size, shape, and other characteristics. I then ask them to hold their stone gently in the palm of one hand and cover it with the palm of the other hand. As we begin our usual breathing exercise, I ask the students to bring their minds back to the stone when they notice their thoughts wandering. When we are done and have opened their eyes, I tell them that the stone is a gift to keep and carry with them.

I have had several students come back to me several years after having taken one of my classes to proudly report that they still carry their stone with them. On occasion, a student has come to me because he has lost his stone and would like a replacement. On one particularly moving occasion, I was presenting a workshop on the use of centering in human services education at a professional conference and had begun to explain to the audience, which included some of my students, that the copresenter, another faculty member in my program, was not there because she was gravely ill. I was finding it difficult to speak because of my own emotions, when one of the students quietly got up from her chair, walked over to me, and handed me a small stone that had been given to her by her teacher, my colleague. This act of kindness on the part of my student was a signal to me that the lessons on self-care had stayed with our students.

Activist Practices.   Activist practices help students become engaged in the community around them, and increase awareness of social issues and advocacy work.

Volunteering, Civic Engagement, and Community Service.   Students in the human services program are required to do a minimum of three hundred hours of voluntary community service work. Two hundred fifty of those hours are in supervised internships, with the additional fifty hours split between two different courses. Inherent in the assignments is the opportunity for and encouragement of reflection about the experience. Students write journal entries about the service-learning experience, how it relates to classroom learning, and the impact it has on their view of the world. Students sometimes express concern about finding time to engage in community service, but when they reflect on their experiences at the end of the semester, they are glad to have done it and have taken away many important lessons.

Advocacy and Bearing Witness.   One assignment I have given to students focuses on their roles as change agents as they become involved in advocacy issues. The students are asked to choose an issue about which they are passionate and identify organizations that advocate around that issue. They are asked to join the organization's "alert" list and actively participate in advocacy, whether in the form of writing letters to legislative leaders, signing petitions, or participating in demonstrations.

As human services professionals, I believe we have a responsibility to be educated about issues that affect the people with whom we work and to work to create change. An overarching theme for students is realizing the impact that they can have on change as they see the results of their advocacy efforts. As with most other assignments, students are asked to keep reflective journals and write papers reflecting on their experiences.

Generative Practice.   Generative practices are designed to foster thoughts and feelings of compassion or devotion.

Metta *or Loving Kindness Meditation.*   In the human services field, *metta,* or loving kindness meditation, can be an insightful tool as we talk about our own biases and judgments or about the fact that we may not always like our coworkers or the people to whom we provide services. I talk about the idea of unconditional positive regard, but it is a difficult concept to grasp. Students often have difficulty separating the person from the behavior, and I have found that loving kindness meditation helps students understand the idea of unconditional positive regard in ways that are far more intuitive.

After explaining the idea of loving kindness meditation with an initial focus on being kind to ourselves, I begin, as always, by asking students to get comfortable in their seats, breathing in and out, being mindful of the sensations of the breathing. As they continue to breathe in and out, I begin to say some of the traditional phrases, asking them to either say them with me, or say them silently: May I be happy . . . may I be healthy . . . may I be safe . . . may I feel peace . . . may I be free of suffering.

I then ask them to think of someone for whom they have unconditional positive regard or respect, usually a mentor, or grandparent, or teacher, or even a child, someone it is easy to think of in loving ways, and as they continue to breath in and out, I repeat the phrases . . . may she be happy . . . may she be healthy . . .

Following the tradition, I then ask them to think of a neutral person, one for whom they have neither strong positive or negative feelings, and allow themselves to feel loving care for this person, repeating the phrases . . . may he feel at peace . . . may he be free from suffering . . .

Moving on to someone they have difficulty with, or strong negative feelings, I ask them to continue breathing in and out, and to say the phrases . . . may he be safe . . . may he be healthy. I tell them if they have difficulty saying those phrases, to begin with "As much as I am able, I wish that you . . . may be happy." I also tell them if this becomes too difficult, to return to the person for whom they feel genuine loving kindness and allow those feelings to come back, and then return to the person with whom they have difficulty.

I then ask them to focus again on their breathing, experiencing the positive feelings. Depending on time and my perception of the students' level of comfort, I may continue the traditional practice of asking the students to send loving kindness out to all beings and to the universe . . . may all beings be safe, happy, healthy, at peace . . .

After teaching the loving kindness meditation, I mention that it can be used as part of a self-care plan by simply focusing on oneself, especially after a difficult day when self-esteem might be at a low point.

Creation Process Practice.   Creation Process Practices use art, music, or writing as a vehicle for reflection and developing mindfulness. An increased awareness of the inner self can be found with creation process practices.

Contemplative Art.   Artistic endeavors are a large part of my personal contemplative practice, and I bring art into the classroom when I can. One activity that seems to have sparked a great deal of interest is the use of mandalas as a form of centering.

A mandala is a design of concentric circles, often used to create a sacred space or to focus attention for meditation. They have been used throughout history, often serving as an instrument of meditation. Swiss psychologist Carl Jung introduced the idea of the mandala to the field of psychology, observing that his own drawing changed as a reflection of his state of mind (Fincher, 1991). Jung (1965) described his insight into the meaning of the circle: "I sketched every morning in a notebook a small circular drawing, a mandala, which seemed to correspond to my inner situation at the time. Only gradually did I discover what the mandala really is: . . . the Self, the wholeness of the personality, which if all goes well is harmonious" (pp. 195–196).

I introduce mandalas as a form of meditation by bringing boxes of colored pencils and copies of printed mandalas to class. Although I teach at the college level, my students are nearly always delighted when I bring colored pencils or markers to class because they know they will be doing something fun. Sometimes the students get to choose the mandala they wish to color; other times everyone gets the same mandala. I ask them to focus on the colors, letting their intuition guide them, and use the mandala as a form of centering. Frances (2007) notes that

> coloring mandalas teaches a certain degree of patience and has a great influence on difficult things becoming simpler. By coloring, people come to accept the orderliness of the mandala, which seems to help their souls create order. It is possible that mandalas intuitively help us to regain our perspective on what really matters in life. . . . The mandala can help to put everything in its proper place, which allows us to see again close up what is truly essential to life [p. 28].

Once everyone is done, students break into small groups to compare their mandalas, reflecting on the similarities and differences. Students manage to find a great deal of insight from the discussion, especially when everyone had the same mandala. They speculate about the use of color, pattern, and design in each other's work. I then ask them to write a reflective journal about the process: "Once you've colored the mandala, reflect on it as a method of centering for you. Did you find yourself 'getting lost' in it? Was it hard to have the discipline to 'stay between the lines'? What did you notice? Is this something you might do again? Why or why not? Anything else you'd like to share?"

Journaling.   Journal writing is an integral part of most courses within the human services program. In some cases, the students are asked to freewrite, and in others, they are given specific prompts to respond to—for example:

- "Write about a difficult situation with an individual client or peer."
- "Write about a situation that left you questioning your competence as a human services worker."
- "Write about how work influences your life."
- "Write about any personal reflections as you observe your growth as a human services worker."

In some cases, students are asked to come up with their own topics. Students have been extremely creative, writing poetry or drawing pictures to convey their thoughts, feelings, and observations.

Conclusion

Over the years as I have integrated contemplative practices into nearly all of the courses I teach, student feedback has validated my initial ideas that learning centering practices in a classroom setting spills over into my students' lives. Time and again, I hear reports from students of the benefits of simple centering activities or keeping a reflective journal. One student was able to avoid the use of medication to treat high blood pressure by developing a meditation practice; another taught centering to her young children as a way to quiet themselves at the end of the day. Other students have reported taking the time to center before tests, after working with a difficult client, or as a way to end the day. Students who have continued their education beyond the associate degree level often stay in touch and continue to report the value of having learned centering activities during their classes here. One benefit I had not anticipated, however, is the spill-over into my own life. As I teach centering activities to my students, I have reinforced my own contemplative practice, and I am able to deal more effectively with the stressors I encounter daily.

While the focus of this chapter has been on human services education, the ideas are applicable to other academic disciplines, especially those in the helping professions, such as nursing and allied health, veterinary sciences, education, and criminal justice. The use of contemplative practices as part of a teaching practice need not be limited to any particular academic discipline and has great potential to improve the lives of students.

In conclusion, the use of contemplative practices in human services education has been a positive experience for students. They learn tools for dealing with the stressors in their lives that they can use immediately and are better able to prevent burnout in their work and personal lives.

References

Azar, S. T. "Preventing Burnout in Professionals and Paraprofessionals Who Work with Child Abuse and Neglect Cases: A Cognitive Behavioral Approach to Supervision." *Journal of Clinical Psychology,* 2000, *56,* 643–663.

Bernstein, G. S. *Human Services? That Must Be So Rewarding.* Baltimore: Brookes, 1999.

Bewley, A. R. *At the Heart of the Matter: Communicating Care in Helping Relationships.* Laconia, N.H.: Harpwell, 2004.

Center for Contemplative Mind in Society. 2002. Retrieved June 16, 2010, from http://www.contemplativemind.org/practices/tree.html.

Dass, R., and Gorman, P. *How Can I Help? Stories and Reflections on Service.* New York: Knopf, 1994.

Figley, C. R. "Compassion Fatigue: Psychotherapists' Chronic Lack of Self Care." *Journal of Clinical Psychology,* 2002, *58, 11,* 1433–1441.

Fincher, S. F. *Creating Mandalas for Insight, Healing, and Self-Expression.* Boston: Shambhala, 1991.

Frances, Z. (ed.). *Mandalas for Meditation.* New York: Sterling, 2007.

Jung, C. *Memories, Dreams, Reflections.* Aniela Jaffe (trans.). Richard and Clara Winston (ed.). New York: Random House, 1965.

Kabat-Zinn, J. *Full Catastrophe Living: Using the Wisdom of Your Body and Mind to Face Stress, Pain and Illness.* New York: Random House, 2005.

Kottler, J., and Zehm, S. *On Being a Teacher: The Human Dimension.* (2nd ed.). Thousand Oaks, Calif.: Corwin Press, 2000.

Selye, H. *The Stress of Life.* New York: McGraw-Hill, 1956.

Seward, B. L. *The Art of Peace and Relaxation Workbook.* Boston: Jones and Bartlett, 2008.

JACQUELINE M. GRISWOLD is department chair of the Human Services Program at Holyoke Community College in Holyoke, Massachusetts.

7

This chapter describes the use of contemplative practice and curriculum design in teaching and learning music.

The Sound of Starting Where You Are: Contemplative Practice and Music Pedagogy

Matthew Ruby Shippee

> *An artist acts with the assumption of innocence within a field of experience.*
> Robert Fripp aphorism for his Guitar Craft seminar students.

Music educators often ask, "How do we best teach students to become experienced musicians so that they can gain all the benefits that come with experience while simultaneously teaching them how to retain their innocence as expressive human beings?" We ask the question because we know that practicing, performing, and experiencing music in a meaningful way depends on more than the accumulation of the right skill set. Musical activity that is expressive transcends the limitations of the tangible. But how does one go about teaching that?

As the progressive rock and genre bending British guitarist Robert Fripp suggests in the quotation at the start of this chapter, experience is tied to context; it comes partly through study and participation in tangible forms of theory, concept, history, and practice within a context. The community college setting is a context in which these things are usually taught, with the goal of equipping students with the right abilities to make music and continue further studies. Every fall semester, beginning community college students are starting off on similar tracks across the country as they encounter Music Theory I and Music History I, join a jazz or concert ensemble, and take private lessons on their primary instruments. Many also

New Directions for Community Colleges, no. 151, Fall 2010 © 2010 Wiley Periodicals, Inc.
Published online in Wiley Online Library (wileyonlinelibrary.com) • DOI: 10.1002/cc.417

work toward and fulfill the requirements of their first college recital performance. These practices, building semester on semester, lead students to become experienced at music in a familiar context. If we take this brief and general depiction to be what Fripp is referring to above as "experience," then what does he mean by "the assumption of innocence"?

I care about the assumption of innocence and offer my interpretation of it for two reasons. First, it steers our attention toward the elusive, abstract aspects of music making. Second, it provides a valuable framework for my practice in the design and execution of a common curriculum that builds experience. We all know what to teach our inexperienced music students, so the juicy part lies in choosing how to teach it.

Fripp carefully worded his axiom to stem from the "assumption," the act of taking on a role or identity. This is important because by the time our students reach us at community college, they are already well past innocence. They have loads of contextual music culture experience that informs and shapes their ideas of what is right or good or valuable in music. As teachers, we often come up against these preconceived notions as we seek to broaden their horizons of musical appreciation beyond whatever it is that might be dominating their experience. Innocence implies that which was before experience. We could say then that innocence regarding music can appear as a childlike fascination with experiencing sound, any kind of sound, without consideration for judgment: for example, the natural feeling of beats and rhythms that goes right through the body and comes out in some form of movement; the ability to explore an instrument and its sonic possibilities free from self-conscious concerns for producing "right" sounds; or, in making sounds, the spontaneous discovery of patterns of sound and the immediate evaluation that the pattern should be repeated or varied in some way. The assumption of innocence is the act of taking on this open, curious, and nonjudgmental way of being in oneself and with music. My students all seem to recognize that the most fabulous things happen for musicians and audiences when this assumption of innocence happens alongside fluid execution of skills based in contextual experience.

Themes in Integrating Contemplative Practice in Music Studies

Contemplative practice as a theme in my teaching and curriculum design has provided a bridge to lead students from a technical-based mind-set regarding music studies to a fuller experience of music and self. As I have integrated contemplative practice more and more into my teaching, I have witnessed students gaining their own ability to take on those aspects of innocence, and they tell me over and over that they love it. Students tell me that this aspect of their studies has enriched their relationship with music, college studies, friends, and family. In our department, if I occasionally forget to organize the preconcert sitting meditation for performing students, they politely and firmly remind me that "we *need* to do that next time!"

One of the important aspects of integrating contemplative practice into higher music education is the emphasis the practice places on individual experience. Students begin to learn to sensitize both their outer and inner listening. They begin to trust their own experience and the inner guidance that can be found in that trust. They begin to trust that they have an individual way of hearing, an individual voice, and a valuable expression to make in music through uncovering that individuality. It seems most natural for this chapter, then, that I have chosen to share informally from my personal experience. I focus on my experience with one class and some teaching techniques I have designed and implemented. I have woven bits of my own story into this chapter as a way of illustrating the individualized and experiential nature of what I have chosen to write about.

When I began teaching ten years ago, I knew intuitively that first and foremost, I wanted to offer my students a whole-person-centered education—a training that would go beyond the necessary aspects of how to make music and into realms of self-knowledge that would transfer to larger questions and understandings of music, self, and living life. I have wanted to guide students toward a sense of wonder at how creativity mysteriously springs from and gives back to life experience. I knew I wanted to guide students in recognizing the difference between music that sufficed to sound like music and music that truly communicated something from within. I wanted our endeavor to be a shared exploration of how musical expression can be learned by sensitive listening and attentive practice of the metamusical aspects of expression, fully integrated with the rest of music studies. Without yet having a name for it, I had already begun to fold contemplative education perspective into my teaching in subtle ways, as I am sure many teachers often do without knowing it.

Over the years and through my own learning about contemplative education, I have come to define contemplative music education as shared mindfulness practice deeply integrated within established music pedagogy. Practicing mindfulness in music is practicing awareness. It is more than just listening because it requires practicing awareness of both external sensing and internal sensing. There are things we know about the awareness of those highly expressive musicians we use as models for performance, regardless of genre. We learn about their unique level of awareness through reports from the performers themselves and, in large part, from our own participatory experience as listeners of their musical performances. We know that exceptionally expressive musicians are highly tuned to the sounds they and others are making in the moment at the same time they are highly tuned to the effect those sounds are having on shaping their interior perception of the moment. The musicians highly experienced in this practice are also empathetic to the shared interior emotional landscape being created among performers and audience members who are present (or even imagined in the case of recordings). Most important, highly expressive musicians recognize a range of nuanced possibilities from which to choose how to respond to all this in sound.

The contemplative approach to music education teaches students that they, like their musical heroes, can follow deep sensitivity into choosing expressive musical responses rather than being limited to reactionary sound statements that are simply habitual and contextually familiar. It is not unlike the intention many meditators have for bringing their sensitive awareness gained by sitting to their communications and interactions when they are not on the cushion.

In my teaching experience, practicing mindfulness activity has taken two general forms. One is the inclusion of contemplative practices such as sitting meditation in class structure. By the nature of our music classroom context and our desire to get instruments in hand and make sounds, this type of activity, while taking on great importance to students, occupies a relatively small amount of time. The other form of mindfulness activity practice relies on the implementation of musical exercises designed to combine traditional and basic elements of music study, such as scales, with elements of contemplative practice. Examples of these exercises are described later in this chapter.

The definition of contemplative music education I work from requires teaching and learning from experience. It is teaching a way of being—being with music and being with oneself and others. I have sought to help my students know the feeling—that wonderful inner experience of freedom and possibility—of making expressive, living music that is connected deeply within them. I have intended to impart a strong value placed on listening, beginning with silence, as the best tool for producing meaningful music—the sound. In my view, teaching creative expression means teaching sensitivity, and teaching sensitivity means teaching mindfulness.

My own background as a musician is primarily as an improviser and a songwriter. For me, creating playfully with sounds and making a lot out of a little came naturally some time right after I learned my second guitar chord when I was twelve years old. As I progressed through my own music studies, I learned both that this sort of thing did not come naturally to all musicians and that others were naturally good at things that were not easy for me. Underlying the differences between us was a common desire to get closer to making music that was inspired and inspiring, though there was little talk in school of what that meant or where it came from. In considering the multiple ways that musicians of various kinds before us had arrived at that goal, I came to a conclusion: "good" music is not absolutely a matter of technique. It is personal expression and communication made through the tools of technique; most important, the level of technique is secondary to the unique blend of technique and expression an especially good musician has created. To blend one's technical talents and expressiveness first requires recognition of one's strengths and limitations. Contemplative education helps me teach students that their balance of strengths and limitations is not to be frowned on for what is lacking. Rather, that balance is essential to the uniqueness of each individual's potentially expressive voice. Embracing and being gentle with oneself regarding both strengths and limitations allows students to drop self-doubts in place of creative possibility. It is not difficult to illustrate examples of this in the work and careers of all sorts of musicians from various styles. I have come to recognize that helping students see vast creative possibility in their own unique set of strengths and limitations is an important part of their coming to understand themselves in music, as well as in life. I have observed many students develop an individual blend of musical technique and expression that seems to grow from this understanding of self.

I did my graduate work in ethnomusicology, which provided much opportunity for seeing ways in which Western music and musical training have often been skewed toward hierarchical models. For example, while growing up in the United States, I learned the usual hierarchies of musical styles, genres, composers, performers, schools, and instruments. I later began to see, much to my surprise, that I had been neatly and quite thoroughly indoctrinated with some of these models. A view of non-Western music cultures and history I learned in ethnomusicology studies did not convince me that I could escape hierarchical structure and patterns, but it did show me some less hierarchical models and that the ones passed down to me were not necessarily more right or true or permanent than others. It was a lesson in nonattachment.

It is both challenging and empowering for growing artists to see such a great many creative and philosophical choices beyond the ready-made structures handed down to them. A sophisticated handling of available choices can develop with an awareness and practice of nonattachment from contemplative practice. As we know, most of our attachments are secured in the background of our being. Through contemplative practice, we learn more clearly what those attachments are, how they are working in us, and ways in which to begin letting go of the attachments. In music studies, contemplative concepts and practices shed light for students on ways in which their attachments to hierarchical views of music and "rights" and "wrongs" may have stunted possibility for truly creative music making. In the process, these students develop personal skills to be carried into all aspects of their lives.

Creative Musicianship

These themes were all at work in my music making and teaching when I arrived at Greenfield Community College in Massachusetts in 2002 to build a new liberal arts–based music program. One of the first things I did was design a two-semester course for music majors titled Creative Musicianship. I essentially packed it with all the things I wished I had learned as an undergraduate music student but instead figured out on my own along the way.

Now in its fourteenth semester, the course has been described by students and others as "the core" and "the heart and soul" of the department. As I have been connecting more in recent years to the contemplative practice movement in higher education, I have been inspired to bring the contemplative aspect of my teaching, in both concept and practice, more to the foreground in this course particularly. In recent semesters, I have incorporated five to fifteen minutes of sitting meditation at the start of class, as well as some basic yoga and contemplative movement. Most significant, I have used mindfulness concepts and vocabulary to tie together musical aspects of the class and to connect the course content to broad and ancient cultural and musical traditions.

My own learning and practice in contemplative education has also influenced my work as chairperson, such that I articulate our department aim to be a balancing of rigorous music preparation with what I call "start where you are" music pedagogy. The approach sums up our clear statement to beginning music majors (partly evident in allowing entrance without audition) that the talents, skills, and knowledge they bring, though often lacking by traditional standards, are the perfect, and only, place to begin from. It also says that their current interests, tastes, goals, and all the rest that they bring with them will be recognized and allowed a place in their academic progression through the program (integrated within private lesson repertoire, for example). We seek to inspire student effort and engagement by connecting goals stated by the student to our expectations for progress rather than demand uniform conformity to set repertoire or set standards.

Our department expectations in all areas demand that students work hard in order to progress and remain in the program, and we explicitly ask them to be open to the potentially challenging aspects of expanding their musical horizons into unfamiliar territory. The contemplative emphasis helps me and other faculty focus on engaging students in these challenges by making it known that we support each student not just as a developing musician but as a transforming individual. The backdrop to this teaching practice as it is rooted in contemplative practice and unfolds in music study can be most easily seen in examples from the Creative Musicianship class.

When people ask me what goes on in Creative Musicianship or what it is I am aiming to convey to students and I have to reply quickly, I often say, "It's about process over product in music making." Some people stop asking questions right then. Others are hooked and cannot stop asking questions. It seems that modern visual art, with its many heroes of process-oriented creation, has had a strong influence in recent decades on postsecondary art education. The same is not true of equivalent modern process-oriented music, as there is scant evidence of its influence on mainstream higher music education. I would speculate that this difference is a reflection of the rigidity with which most musicians and music educators unthinkingly perpetuate the importance of music as an object or end product. It seems that getting something to sound "good" or "right" according to some expected standard is often the gauge for success. Whereas art education commonly addresses the process of art making as a blend of interior and exterior sensation, music education remains focused primarily on the external sensory product.

Contemplative practices ranging from yoga to meditation are frequently taught to be lifelong, ongoing practices—that is, something to be done for the value of doing it, not for accomplishment of an end point. Teachers of these practices often remark that focusing on the outcome from doing postures or sitting can almost ensure that such an outcome will not be met. They advise to be in the moment, be with the mind, and be with the body. Translating this way of thinking and practicing opens up a world of possibility for teaching music. Many music students are so concerned with whether they sound "right" (the product) that they forget themselves and forget to pay attention to that wonderful process of playing with the sounds, expressing their selves through sound. Sadly, some music students who lose touch with the process also lose touch with the joy of playing that set them on the music path in the first place, eventually quitting music studies in frustration or gradually quitting music after college. Teaching students to watch themselves and to be mindful of their music process empowers them to choose and create a personal relationship with music. I have seen students have their challenges with practicing and their ideas about commercial success be completely transformed by turning their attention to the process of music making as a lifelong practice.

I have found that Creative Musicianship students, even those who are uneasy at first with the idea, are most often compelled to give themselves over to process over product when I frame the endeavor in experiential terms. I ask students to hear music as sound, beyond knowing labels like *genres, harmony,* or *instruments.* After this initial break with that level of attachment, I ask them to try exploring sounds. Just explore and experience the senses, external and internal, that come with exploring. They report feeling fear, nervousness, uncertainty, and lack of confidence. I guide them to become more comfortable with these feelings as experiences to go toward with an attitude of curiosity. I ask them to become aware of what it feels like when, after a period of exploration, they discover something: a sound they like, something that works for them musically and emotionally in the context, something exciting in any way. They love that feeling because it is the eureka, aha, payoff moment. I guide students to embrace their own experience of the relationship between exploration and discovery, between risk taking and payoff. Most of my students have inherently gravitated toward this experience once they are pointed in the direction. It is the same root experience of revelation that began their fascination with music, and it is what their musical heroes seem to be able to elicit in listeners. As we practice throughout the course of the school year, some students begin to emerge with their own voice or style that is clearly linked to their own unique flow of exploration and discovery.

Contemplative-Based Musical Activities

Once the foundation principles of process over product and experiential exploration and discovery are in place, I strive to help students build their practice in this realm through a range of contemplative-based musical activities in class. The following sections address some of these class activities, with brief descriptions of how they are carried out.

The Syllabus.   An important aspect of the contemplative education model in my experience is teaching by example. When we offer ourselves as an example of practicing the lesson we aim to teach, we convey a completeness of the what, why, and how of the lesson that goes beyond teaching by description. With this in mind, I designed the syllabus for Creative Musicianship with a semester outline that leaves blank space for each week's class content and assignments. The outline introduction reads: "Corresponding to the nature of this course, class activities and assignments will be specifically determined in a spontaneous and improvisatory manner. This will allow maximum flexibility for all of us to shape the direction and content of the class cooperatively."

With every new group of fall semester students, I see more than a few surprised looks on student faces when we review this part of the syllabus on the first day. Some are surprised with enthusiasm for the idea, some are slightly confused, and a few look as if they have hit the jackpot of easy courses. While many seriously engaged teachers adjust and adapt their course outlines in response to students each semester, it is a powerful thing to go this extra step and let students know they are co-creating this course. It is an extra step of in-the-moment engagement and risk on the part of the teacher. This aspect of my syllabus is the first lesson for students in what our class is about and how seriously I am committed to its ideals as their teacher.

The students who may struggle with the class at first are usually the ones who mistakenly thought it would be easy. There is nothing easy about being asked to engage meaningfully in open-ended creative endeavors. My goal for teaching mindfulness in self-awareness and self-knowledge leads me to ask students to do this kind of difficult, energy-consuming reflective and thoughtful engagement. A section regarding the course philosophy reads:

> This class asks students to grow in their ability to think for themselves and express something personal of themselves through words and music; it asks students to connect with their individual sources and processes of creative expression, rather than conform to something pre-set or pre-determined.

This work is not easy, and it is not something that can be learned by follow-ing a set of step-by-step, "connect the dots" style of performance assignments or writing assignments. Assignments will be intentionally open-ended such that every student will have to confront the difficult task of doing indepen-dent, personal thinking and expression. Full engagement by students with the class work on this level will help students become more fully expressive and creative musicians.

One of the ways in which I guide students in learning how to practice this level of self-reflective engagement is to require that the weekly blank space be filled in with two things: the assignment for the week and what our class activities were for the week. I always involve students in deter-mining the direction of each class meeting such that none of us knows in advance exactly where it will go. I also refrain from finalizing assignments in advance of class meetings in order to ensure that out-of-class class work builds on the class and leads students forward toward the shared direction that we all sense things are headed in.

Sitting Meditation.   The core elements of this course that connect mindful sensitivity to music making were present in its early incarnations. One major change that took place three years ago, after four years of teach-ing it, was the inclusion of sitting meditation during class, usually near the start of our class meeting. Thanks to an opportunity to attend the Center for Contemplative Mind in Society's Summer Session on Contemplative Curriculum Development at Smith College in 2007, I was able to see my way to adding this important activity into the course structure.

My experience with sitting meditation in class has been profound. I am continuously reminded that most of our students are hungry for this ave-nue of self knowledge and life enhancement. Most of my students, once acquainted with the practice, are especially enthusiastic about this part of the course, and many report that they use some form of sitting on their own in musical and nonmusical contexts. The class experience carries over into other classes and department activities. For example, many students are eager to organize pre-concert group sits in a quiet place after all concert sound checks and warm-ups are done.

For me, the greatest challenge in implementing sitting meditation has been making it feel accessible for my students, who often do not have any-thing like it in their family or social backgrounds. I have experienced two kinds of initial resistance from some students: one is based on ideological and cultural difference and inherited skepticism of the unfamiliar, and the other is resistance to being still and quiet with oneself. The latter is almost always eased by teaching that resistance is part of the practice, with gentle-ness and nonjudgment as our means for being with that resistance. I am able to make a bridge here by teaching students the value of gentleness and nonjudgment as it relates to the inner critic they all know so well in regard to trying to make music. I have heard many students say that this has transformed their relationship with that inner critical voice and empowered them to feel freer and to take more risks in music.

I invite students to practice nonattachment to their familiar views and methods of operation in life as it relates to music in a number of ways. One especially notable way I have found to open students to an unfamiliar sitting practice is to present it as a mind-altering activity and make a bridge between it and another mind-altering activity they know of: drug use. With so many musical heroes having gone down the road of using drugs and ending up dead or creatively incapacitated, there is vivid illustration for presenting the need for alternatives. Through guided discussion, I allow students to reflect on and to realize together why drugs have been connected to music making. The usual stand-out reasons include the desire to experience (there is that word: *experience*) creative flow and creative highs; the desire to transform one's "headspace" in order to discover new sounds in music creation; and to self-medicate insecurity and stage fright. As the picture of all this begins to take shape and we examine drug use on the one hand and meditation and mindfulness practice on the other, students begin to see that they might be able to have everything they want if they are willing to engage in self-affirming practice rather than ultimately self-destructive short-cuts. I am inspired by how many of my students truly understand this and make choices while at the college that will have a positive impact on their lives ahead.

Mbira.   Our main music classroom is quite large, making it easy to arrange fifteen students in the large seated circle that is our customary configuration when not playing music as a group. At our first or second class meeting, I usually bring along some unusual instrument. Often it is an mbira (pronounced "embeera") a metal-keyed instrument originating in Zimbabwe that is played with thumbs. I play a bit on the instrument and hand it to the next person in the circle, asking that person to play for a minute or so before passing it on. The mbira has been new to every student in my classes thus far. Even more significant is the new experience of being asked to play music on an unfamiliar instrument, one that they do not already "know" or "play." As the mbira makes its way around the circle, impressions are formed about the instrument, the experience of playing it, listening to it, and personalities in the classroom. I do not comment or ask questions until everyone has played.

When I ask students about the experience of playing, they speak of feeling nervous and uncertain but liking the newness of what they feel and hear. They also speak of exploring the instrument for possibilities in making sound. When I ask about the experience of listening, students relay details of sonic explorations and surprising discoveries that they heard from each other and say that they were influenced by what they heard played before their turn (to imitate it or not) and that they could perceive aspects of nervousness, boldness, playfulness, and other emotive traits in each other's playing.

It is quite amazing how much music, in the deep sense of musical sound communication, can happen in this circle of people who are encountering and producing sound on an instrument for the first time. As these impressions are noted and described by students, I keep track and eventually reflect them back to students as examples of the musical aspects we will be pursuing in class. I reinforce the necessity of their music theory and private lesson technical studies before explaining that our goal for this class is to deemphasize those aspects of music and emphasize playing music beyond the limitations inherent in being tied too tightly to theory and technique. The mbira challenges students to do and say something with sound without being able to rely on known theory and technique. Because there are no habitual, easy, or familiar theoretical or technical pathways to follow, the task requires a mind-set of being completely attentive to the moment: attentive to what they hear while playing, what they want to hear, what they feel, their balance of strengths and limitations, and the unavoidable exploration of sound possibilities. In later weeks I challenge students with the much harder task of approaching their known and familiar instruments with this same mind-set of deep and sensitive attentiveness to possibility. The hardest part is letting go of what they know.

Playing One Note. Playing one note is the basic starting point for asking students to play two notes, or three notes, or one scale against a drone, or one melodic phrase, and so on. This exercise is built on the idea that strictly limiting the set of possibilities normally associated with theory, technique, and repertoire forces students to focus on another set of possibilities that is more often ignored, or at least left to the realm of unconscious impulse. The set of possibilities I ask students to engage with primarily are those found in the first chapter of any introductory music appreciation book. The basic elements of music—pitch, dynamics, timbre, and such—are basic in concept but infinitely complex in execution. In this realm of possibilities lie the most accessible and powerful means for expressiveness for musicians with wide-ranging sets of strengths and limitations.

In most corners of music education, budding musicians are expected to simply assimilate an ability in this area of music making through listening and playing. It is an ability I often hear lacking in college graduates from even highly regarded institutions. Slowing down and taking detours from commonly accepted pedagogical practices into these areas of music making can be frowned on because in many cases, music study is directed toward a measurable end point, something to be completed and heard as a successful product or checked off the list of advanced skill acquisition.

When I ask students to go home and practice playing one note for five minutes three times per day for one week, I am taking them on a detour. I am asking them to become mindful of their music making by seriously considering and exploring the range of possibilities for creating musical sound with one note. I guide them to use dynamics (volume) and various changes in dynamics (steps, gradations, leaps). I guide them to explore timbre possibilities and consider how different timbres can take on relational values between each other in the context of playing. I suggest they explore staccato and legato phrasing and rhythmic possibilities and variations of rhythms. I ask them to sense how combinations of these can say angry, joyful, depressed, or grieving, for example. I ask them to explore silence and various densities of sound. I ask them to explore contrast and think about how form can develop through statements, repetition, development of ideas stated, and return to repetition.

The possibilities grow as we add more notes, eventually allowing melodies moving in steps or leaps. I will state again that this practice is done in conjunction with the other valuable and more conventionally accepted music studies required of majors. It is the blend of both types of study that I see so well equipping students to recognize and choose from a palette of musical and expressive possibilities.

Free Improvisation Playing.   The culmination of these and many other exercises in Creative Musicianship for students is playing free improvisation as a group. I define *free* differently for students according to context because it is hard to make a case for any type of playing being absolutely free. Sometimes I specifically ask everyone to play within a form while avoiding any known scales, harmony, or rhythmic patterns as a way to prioritize exploration of intentionally unstructured sounds within the group. At other times, I ask students to begin without any preplanned structure of any kind and allow them to discover structure collectively, adhering only to a shared intention to genuinely explore and discover. And at still other times I ask for improvisation to be played in different ways against drones or accompanied by a particular time signature.

The most important part of free improvising is that students are practicing mindfulness in listening, feeling, and interacting while participating in a collective process of exploration and discovery. I have recently partnered with one of our college painting teachers and begun class collaborations of improvisational music with improvisational painting in an open gallery space on campus. It has been instructive for me to witness music students as they witness passersby stopping to express their great enthusiasm for the sounds being created. It is telling and inspiring for us all to see people so moved by music that is rooted in contemplative practice and to recognize that students of contemplative music education are able to make unscripted connections with listeners in that way.

Conclusion

Returning once again to the Robert Fripp refrain, music "is the assumption of innocence within a field of experience." From my point of view, the field of experience is an individual's contextual learning and development that come with conventional music pedagogy in theory, technique, standard repertoire development, and multitudes of nonpedagogical influences. It is experience in acquiring musical knowledge, vocabulary, coded framework, and points of reference without which musical communication would not exist. The "assumption of innocence" represents the ability possessed by good improvisers and expressive performers for accessing and foregrounding their musically inexperienced emotional and expressive self in the process of music creation.

Through my teaching, I have become convinced that innocence can be learned and practiced by students as well and as seriously as experience. After an innocent early stage of life, we must learn how to assume innocence through a kind of access to ourselves, presumably with greater and greater depth and agility from practice over time. Contemplative practice provides that access and has formed the foundation for my approach to teaching music because it emphasizes three main points for students:

- *Start where you are.* The balance of strength and limitations each student brings to music study represents a part of his or her potential for uniqueness. In combination with a diligent work ethic, most students guided in this way can find lasting rewards in their musical pursuits, regardless of future academic or professional tracks. Some go on to excel in academic and professional music settings in large part because they were invited to music study in this way.
- *Explore and discover.* Many students find an irresistible thrill in being encouraged to engage firsthand with the experience of taking risks in music. To give students permission to inhabit their passionately emotional and curious selves is to reconnect them with the source of their initial love of music. This leads to a view of musical process as intrinsically valuable, deemphasizing musical product as the sole measure for success.
- *Music is life.* In the way I teach music, one of my goals is to continuously connect our musical endeavor to how we live our larger lives. I ask students to know themselves as sensitive and responsive musicians with the ability to communicate meaningfully with their audience. I have found that many students are eager to make bridges between that and their process of figuring out a paradigm by which to live their lives. It is a privilege to be so closely involved with so many thoughtful students engaged in this work.

MATTHEW RUBY SHIPPEE, a professional musician, is chairperson and professor in the music department at Greenfield Community College in Greenfield, Massachusetts.

8

This chapter offers a faculty development model based on contemplative practice within a multiple-campus community college system.

Offering Reflection to an Organization

Ann Faulkner, Guy Gooding

From 1998 to 2008, the Dallas County Community College District (DCCCD) offered its employees a variety of options for formation, a type of reflective practice. The district encompasses ten locations, seven of them independently accredited colleges. Formation is based primarily on Parker Palmer's model for Circles of Trust as described in *A Hidden Wholeness* (2004). Palmer is a writer on issues of education, community, and spirituality who was a consultant to the DCCCD, visiting twice during each academic year from 1998 to 2003. During that time, formation was introduced through short retreats called samplers and took root as longer retreats as a form of staff development offered to employees by the district's office of staff and organizational development and as a campus-based activity supported by local staff development funds. Palmer described formation as a type of inner work offered in retreats of various lengths led by specially prepared facilitators. This chapter describes those programs and shares suggestions for creating similar programs on other college campuses.

How a Public Institution of Higher Education Can Introduce Reflective Practice to Employees

Building a context in which institutions can offer inner work to employees is crucial. In 1997, Bill Wenrich was chancellor of the seven-college DCCCD; he was a widely recognized leader in the field of community college development and was respected and admired within the district. He was a strong supporter of the vice chancellor of professional and

NEW DIRECTIONS FOR COMMUNITY COLLEGES, no. 151, Fall 2010 © 2010 Wiley Periodicals, Inc.
Published online in Wiley Online Library (wileyonlinelibrary.com) • DOI: 10.1002/cc.418

development affairs, Bill Tucker, who had been casting about for a way to respond to the needs of an aging faculty whose long tenure seemed to portend decreased energy and increased resistance to innovation. He was intrigued with Palmer's ideas of returning heart to teaching, so he organized a group to meet with Palmer and Fetzer Institute staff in Kalamazoo, Michigan, in August 1997. This exploratory delegation was composed of two dozen people: a trustee, top administrators, and professional association leaders from the DCCCD, along with representatives from our largest urban school district, a suburban school district, and Dallas's business and nonprofit sectors.

The diversity and depth of the exploratory group were essential to the subsequent dissemination of formation throughout the DCCCD. By including so many of the decision makers and stakeholders in the initial meeting, Wenrich and Tucker had developed a significant cohort with shared firsthand experience of Palmer's ideas and the practice of inner work in community. Although some of the initial partners were unable to participate directly in the DCCCD's subsequent reflective retreats, all have remained friends and advocates.

In February 1999, a group of faculty and administrators from Richland College, one of the seven colleges in the DCCCD, traveled to Kalamazoo to begin a Fetzer Institute–funded process of exploring the application of formation principles to classroom practice. Each had committed to writing a short essay about their individual experiences at the four-day retreat to be gathered in a monograph, *To Teach with Soft Eyes* (Garcia, 2000), published by the League for Innovation in the Community College. Faculty participants had also agreed to develop a course with a mind-body emphasis, and the administrators agreed to integrate some aspect of their learning into their work. Guidance for the writing was supplied by English professor Rica Garcia, who used her expertise in composition and her personal experience with reflective practice to develop a plan for "writing in community."

A decade later, it is clear that the Fetzer group contributed significantly to setting a course for excellence culminating in Richland College's being named the first community college recipient of a Malcolm Baldrige National Quality Award in 2005, as well as developing into the U.S. college with the most far-reaching formation program. Richland's president of three decades, Steve Mittelstet, expressed the need for wholeness in individuals, organizations, and communities:

> Whole organizations invite whole people to have the courage to be authentic in taking responsible risks to help students learn. Dysfunctional organizations, where systems and processes fail, for which unwitting players are frequently punished, cause faculty, staff, and students to "play it safe," "go through the motions," "get the credential," keeping their vulnerable souls tucked safely away elsewhere. So leaders must work with faculty and staff who, in turn, work with students both to create well-functioning, safe,

supportive, welcoming institutions and to help individuals re-learn how to engage spirit-mind-body more fully. It is challenging enough to engage faculty meaningfully in ongoing and cyclical organizational processes. It is even more challenging to help spirit-cautious adults, broken by dysfunction in family, society, and institutional life, to reconnect with and engage their authentic selves in their work. Yet it must be done if there is to be hope for the existence of whole, healthy communities on a whole, healthy planet [personal communication to the authors, 2009].

Some Factors to Consider in Introducing Reflective Practice to a College Community

- Involve the right people from the beginning: the trustees, chief institutional administrators, and professional association leaders. Having formation trickle up is not impossible, but without the support of senior leadership, faculty and staff who take the initiative often become isolated and disheartened.
- Keep the involvement voluntary, emphasizing the point that participation does not indicate endorsement (and that deciding not to participate does not constitute a repudiation of the practice), and that not proceeding with the project is a possibility.
- As an initial activity, do something atypical in a special place. It is not necessary to travel to Michigan, but it is essential not to present a plan of action in a regular business meeting. Getting away, experiencing reflection firsthand, and having some private time to think are critical ingredients in learning about formation.

How to Implement a Program of Formation at a College

The initial implementation of formation in the DCCCD had two important dimensions: preparing facilitators and offering two-year retreat series. To follow up on the enthusiasm generated by the August 1997 trip to Fetzer, the district staff and organizational development office offered a pilot retreat series beginning in 1998. This retreat was open only to faculty, and the invitation made clear that only those who could commit to attending eight retreats meeting quarterly for two years should apply. By funding an employee's self-development, the institution gains considerable gratitude from employees, which can be critical in building trust and mutual respect.

We learned from the initial retreat group that using an urban retreat site does not provide the best incentive to solitary reflection, so the next retreats were held in an affordable location outside our county. We also learned that two nights proved more workable than three. Two dozen participants became the target size for retreat groups; that number provided a workable size for mutually supportive individual work.

Preparing local facilitators to lead retreats was another critical part of the initial implementation of formation in the DCCCD. Finding leaders of reflective practice among educators is not so easy as it might sound because many teacher "scripts" interfere with introspection and open-ended reflection. The six who were initially chosen included several faculty members and a few administrators and community members. During that first semester, the six met frequently as a group to try out poems, stories, and activities to stimulate reflection during a retreat. They took turns preparing an offering, sharing it with the group, and getting their reflective feedback. This proved a vital learning experience because they all needed practice in working with the tension of offering experiences that relate to a theme without expecting facilitator-determined outcomes. They also did some group planning for the agendas of sampler retreats. They decided on cofacilitation because it offered many advantages: more people could get involved; as newcomers to facilitation of reflective practice, they would have the comfort and assistance of a colleague in the circle; and group members would have some diversity in facilitation styles.

The first locally facilitated DCCCD retreat series sponsored by the district office of staff and organizational development began in fall 1999. That group consisted of about twenty faculty members and instructional administrators and was cofacilitated by Ann Faulkner, a recently retired DCCCD faculty member and coauthor of this chapter, and another facilitator-in-training, Larry Spencer, a minister and community organizer. The mentoring of senior formation facilitator Marianne Novak Houston was close and significant. Since she is a master at open, honest questions, her phone consultations were wonderful formation practice, as well as helpful guidance for the facilitators-in-preparation.

Experience from the earliest retreats showed that community college retreat participants naturally used ways of work not so much from their classrooms (though the impulse to teach was strong) as from their departmental meetings, which were characterized more by debate, self-protection, and confrontation than reflection and deep listening. Quickly, the new facilitators perceived the need for a written document that would convey the group norms so that the facilitators would not have to lecture about how to interact with each other. Our guidelines were grounded in Palmer's *The Courage to Teach* (1998) and focused on listening to ourselves and others, offering clearness committees for discernment (a practice borrowed from the Society of Friends for seeking clarity about personal dilemmas), and making thematic use of seasonal metaphors through stories, poems, journaling, and reflective silence. Since then, the document has been revised into the currently used touchstones. The version developed by the Center for Renewal and Wholeness in Higher Education contains eleven items:

1. *Be 100% present, extending and presuming welcome.* Set aside the usual distractions of things undone from yesterday, things to do tomorrow. Bring all of yourself to the work. We all learn most effectively in spaces

that welcome us. Welcome others to this place and this work, and presume that you are welcomed as well.

2. *Listen deeply.* Listen intently to what is said; listen to the feelings beneath the words. As Quaker writer Douglas Steere puts it, "Holy listening—to 'listen' another's soul into life, into a condition of disclosure and discovery—may be almost the greatest service that any human being ever performs for another." Listen to yourself as well as to others. Strive to achieve a balance between listening and reflecting, speaking and acting.

3. *It is never "share or die."* You will be invited to share in pairs, in small groups, and in the large group. The invitation is exactly that. *You* will determine the extent to which you want to participate in our discussions and activities.

4. *No fixing.* Each of us is here to discover our own truths, to listen to our own inner teacher, to take our own inner journey. We are *not* here to set someone else straight, or to help right another's wrong, to "fix" what we perceive as broken in another member of the group.

5. *Suspend judgment.* Set aside your judgments. By creating a space between judgments and reactions, we can listen to the other, and to ourselves, more fully.

6. *Identify assumptions.* Our assumptions are usually invisible to us, yet they undergird our worldview. By identifying our assumptions, we can then set them aside and open our viewpoints to greater possibilities.

7. *Speak your truth.* You are invited to say what is in your heart, trusting that your voice will be heard and your contribution respected. Your truth may be different from, even the opposite of, what another person in the circle has said. Yet speaking your truth is simply that—it is not debating with, or correcting, or interpreting what another has said. *Own* your truth by remembering to speak only for yourself. Using the first person "I" rather than "you" or "everyone" clearly communicates the personal nature of your expression.

8. *Respect silence.* Silence is a rare gift in our busy world. After someone has spoken, take time to reflect without immediately filling the space with words. This applies to the speaker as well—be comfortable leaving your words to resound in the silence, without refining or elaborating on what you have just said. This process allows others time to fully listen before reflecting on their own reactions.

9. *Maintain confidentiality.* Create a safe space by respecting the confidential nature and content of discussions held in the formation circle. Allow what is said in the circle to remain there.

10. *When things get difficult, turn to wonder.* If you find yourself disagreeing with another, becoming judgmental, or shutting down in defense, try turning to wonder: "I wonder what brought her to this place." "I wonder what my reaction teaches me." "I wonder what he's feeling right now."

11. *Practice slowing down.* As Thomas Merton and others were already cautioning by the 1960s, even simply the speed of modern life can cause violent damage to the soul. By intentionally practicing slowing down we strengthen our ability to extend non-violence to others—and to ourselves.

We typically ask participants in each retreat to choose one or more touchstones with personal relevance to affirm to the circle; in this way, they become shared values. Retreat participants rate the touchstones as one of the most valuable parts of their formation experience because they find these guidelines useful throughout their lives. They are sometimes used to guide class discussions, often undergird new ways of interacting with colleagues and family members, and sometimes even transform departmental meetings and inspire college value statements.

Selection and preparation of facilitators is crucial to the success of a college's formation efforts. Since 2001, the Center for Renewal and Wholeness in Higher Education (CRWHE), housed at Richland College since 2008, has worked to prepare facilitators through retreats, mentoring, and collaboration with other facilitators. The CRWHE is unequaled in providing principled, individualized preparation to facilitators chosen by their colleges to design and deliver their formation plan. The CRWHE staff welcomes the opportunity to consult with colleges about selecting facilitators-in-preparation because choosing those to be prepared as facilitators requires care and insight. Indeed, the CRWHE supports the concept of a diverse formation team, including facilitators to help bring formation to the college.

These experiences suggest several important steps in implementing a program of formation on a college campus:

1. Arrange for an initial formation retreat to help identify a team of facilitators to be prepared and determine if formation is a fit for the college.
2. Support the preparation of facilitators while beginning to offer a retreat series, perhaps involving facilitation from the CRWHE or a prepared facilitator at a nearby college.
3. While maintaining the voluntary participation requirement, make every effort to involve key stakeholders from the various constituencies at the college.

How the Program Might Develop After the Initial Phase

As the DCCCD formation movement began to enter its maturity, many new programs came into existence, and the original programs evolved and changed. One of the most significant changes came from faculty members who recommended that future formation groups be open to all employee groups—faculty, administrators, and support staff—and that both full- and part-time employees be eligible to attend. As faculty shared their observations about the formation retreats with colleagues, they uncovered serious differences in attitude toward staff development among the various employee groups. They had not realized that while they felt entitled to take some time for their own professional development, support staff supervisors often refused permission to attend staff development activities or approved only mandatory or narrowly focused job skills workshops.

The value of formation was clear to retreat participants. They offered feedback at the end of each retreat session, consistently revealing a sense of personal growth, of coming into one's own through the reflection and exploration, and of deep appreciation to the DCCCD for extending the offer of this form of professional development. Participants indicated that they felt increased satisfaction with their work and the balance of their personal and professional lives. They felt more effective, better able to deal with change, more comfortable in high-stress situations, and better able to accept or delegate authority to solve problems.

Another measure of the value of formation was to be seen in its diffusion throughout the DCCCD. Richland College had been an early adopter, and its formation program was flourishing with the preparation of local facilitators from diverse personal backgrounds as well as diverse job titles and responsibilities. Most of the other colleges developed their own plans for retreats, which were typically supported by a combination of campus and district funds.

The district staff and organizational development office (SOD) also sponsored a district-wide formation group, Formation at Work. The other retreats focused on seasonal themes without making specific references to students or instruction. The Formation at Work group included participants from all locations and a great variety of work groups. The focus of the half-day retreats was on the worker self. Consistent with touchstone 4 about "no fixing," the group avoided focusing on how to remedy district problems. However, our individual reflections in this supportive setting became the catalyst for plans for the 2002 district conference day.

In addition to ongoing retreat series sponsored by the district office and the campus-based retreats, the SOD began to underwrite the facilitation of support activities for both facilitators and participants in completed series. Deepening the Journey retreats, generally attended by twenty to twenty-five participants, were held twice each semester and met from two until eight o'clock in the home of the facilitator. Even after district funding diminished, the group continued to meet, with facilitators volunteering their time and participants paying for their meals. Participants in the two original retreat groups continue to fund their own quarterly meetings to deepen their reflective practice in the setting they have found supportive for a decade. All who have been introduced to clearness committees are welcome to request such a session when they want to explore a significant life issue. All of the facilitators help in locating committee members and convening such groups when asked.

The "deepening" retreats provided an opportunity for new facilitators to practice developing agendas and to cofacilitate with seasoned facilitators. Support for DCCCD facilitators also included periodic day-long meetings in a facilitator's home, where facilitators-in-preparation could practice their skills and be introduced to new aspects of inner work.

Because the director of SOD and coauthor of this chapter, Guy Gooding, had been prepared as a facilitator, formation had considerable impact on all the programs SOD offered. New employee orientation was one program that was entirely revamped to reflect the principles of appreciative inquiry and formation. The ceremony recognizing award winners from the annual district conference day was also changed along similar lines.

Perhaps the most broadly felt impact of formation was made on the annual district conference day itself in 2002. Conference day brings together more than two thousand faculty members and administrators from all the locations of the DCCCD for a day of professional development. That year, chancellor Bill Wenrich had just resigned, and the board of trustees was in the process of selecting a new chancellor. The Formation at Work group made a proposal to prepare for conference day by having focus groups on every campus identify the major issues of celebration and needed growth within the DCCCD. The campus input led to the identification of discussion topics: the spirit of the DCCCD, diversity, innovation, student-centered learning, and relationship-centered community. Not surprisingly, the areas of celebration were also the issues that challenged us to grow. Conference day group discussions on these topics were facilitated by volunteers with formation experience using a locally developed version of author and organizational consultant Meg Wheatley's "simple conversations" guidelines in *Turning to One Another* (2002). The guidelines emphasize acknowledging our equality, remaining curious, becoming better listeners, slowing down, and expecting conversation to be messy. Feedback about that conference day affirmed an experience that was unique and electric. Involvement in authentic conversation about the self-identified most important issues proved a vivid, productive experience.

In the early days, evaluation of formation consisted of surveying participants about how the event could have been better, modifying the next retreat accordingly. In the middle phase, as it became clear that formation was having a major impact on the lives of retreat participants and on the way the institution conducted business, a more thoughtful and comprehensive approach to evaluation seemed in order. Colleagues at the Center for Courage and Renewal (CCR) had piloted a pre-post assessment instrument with retreat participants, and the DCCCD facilitators replicated that process. Results were similar: formation renews teachers' commitment to teaching, it improves their teaching, and they become more reflective and more balanced in their lives. But the CCR instrument was long and telegraphed the desirable direction for change so clearly that it made some respondents uncomfortable, so we decided to stop using it and to convene more focus groups to hear about the outcomes of retreat series. The focus groups gave similar clear indications of the nature of change experienced in formation. Developing a value-neutral, easily administered instrument for assessing heartfelt change proved too great a task with the available resources. The CRWHE staff is currently collaborating on finding existing instruments that might be useful in these measurements.

Some observations from this stage of the reflective journey include the following:

- The maturational period of a formation movement in a collegiate workplace may be varied, challenging, and unpredictable in its approaches to growth.
- One challenge is to make sure that while responding to legitimate local needs, the new programs remain true to the touchstones and the essential requirement of offering voluntary individual work in a safe, supportive community.
- The principles of formation are useful to organizational development work, and the availability of a large group of formation-seasoned staff constitutes a valuable resource for new program implementation.
- Evaluation of formation is important, and the difficulties relating to an evaluation of the individual's changes through reflection and inner work are considerable.

How to Respond Reflectively in Times of Recession

In recent years, many programs have received decreasing administrative support, including reduced funding, and not surprisingly, the DCCCD formation program has been reduced. The only college that had an independent budget for formation was Richland, so its ongoing programs of day retreats and series were not affected, but the campus-based programs supported by the SOD can no longer be funded.

Since this budget contraction came a decade after the start of the formation journey, hundreds of district employees have already had an experience with this reflective practice. Self-funded formation is likely to continue with volunteer facilitation, but with retirements on the increase, formation will tend to become more a thing that those of longer tenure do. Developing new sources of funding is a challenge, as is finding ways to keep new employees aware of the formation movement and how it might affect their lives as educators.

The involvement of formation principles in interactions with students has not been the focus of the DCCCD program, but participants whose lives have been changed by reflection and refraining from fixing inevitably find themselves incorporating aspects of the touchstones in what they do, so more and more students are coming into contact with these ideas. As formation participants move into administrative roles, a change in the tone of departmental meetings and office interactions can be felt. Having the executive officer of the college support formation is the best way to ensure its stability, but even in the absence of budgetary or philosophical support, those who have experience with the tenets of formation find ways to bring them into organizational and personal life. The value of reflective practice is real, and even without programs for dissemination, formation will have an effect on the lives of DCCCD employees. We offer three observations about this phase of formation in the DCCCD:

1. *Soft is hard.* Even in times of abundance, some members of the academy avoid anything "touchy-feely." Some who did not participate in formation in the DCCCD came to stereotype formation as soft, not rigorous, and as self-indulgent rather than an investment in education. Starting, sustaining, or maintaining on a shoestring a significant program of reflective practice in higher education is not for the faint of heart, especially in times of scarcity.

2. *Starting a program of formation without funding or administrative support is not impossible.* Grassroots work such as book discussions, particularly among faculty, who have more control over their time use, can provide an important starting point for reflective practice. As other chapters in this volume clearly show, a variety of reflective practices can be useful without administrative support or notice.

3. *Finding a balance between the institution's need to inculcate policy and to teach skills and the employees' needs to find ways to grow internally is challenging.* Allowing the pendulum of staff development offerings to swing from one extreme to the other is less effective than finding ways to offer both at the same time.

References

Garcia, R. (ed.) *To Teach with Soft Eyes.* Phoenix: League for Innovation in the Community College, 2000.

Palmer, P. J. *The Courage to Teach: Exploring the Inner Landscape of a Teacher's Life.* San Francisco: Jossey-Bass, 1998.

Palmer, P. J. *A Hidden Wholeness: The Journey Toward an Undivided Life.* San Francisco: Jossey-Bass, 2004.

Wheatley, M. J. *Turning to One Another: Simple Conversations to Restore Hope to the Future.* San Francisco: Berrett-Koehler, 2002.

ANN FAULKNER *is professor emerita of reading in the Dallas County Community College District.*

GUY GOODING *is the former director of staff and organizational development in the Dallas County Community College District.*

This chapter describes the role of vocation in career exploration and first-year orientation courses.

Vocatio: The Importance of Exploring an Ancient Concept for Community College Students

Clifford "Kip" Scott

Each year, students come to American college and university campuses to embark on a new journey in their lives. For most, it is an opportunity to acquire the knowledge and skills necessary to pursue careers in their chosen fields. For some, it is an experience encompassing much more than just acquiring knowledge and skills. For others, higher education is a life-changing event. Regardless, most students' primary purpose is to prepare for some form of life's work.

Institutions of higher education usually provide students with a variety of opportunities to help them find and prepare for this life's work. Numerous terms are used to describe the process: *career exploration, career development, career counseling,* and *life mapping.* The process usually involves a battery of career tests to determine the student's personality, interests, skills, and abilities. The results are compiled and compared and generally result in a personal career profile suggesting the careers the individual might pursue. This becomes a rather logical, scientific way to discover and find one's life work.

Many of the ideas for the Student Success Initiative explored in this chapter came from my doctoral studies in Colorado State University's Community College Leadership Program. I am forever grateful to my colleagues and the faculty at the university for sharing their ideas and experiences with me.

And so students come to campuses all across the country to begin the task of finding a life's work that will satisfy their basic needs of living and, the hope is, give them a sense of meaning and purpose. Most of this effort focuses on the traditional approaches. These approaches are not wrong; they just do not go far enough.

Turning to *Vocatio*

In 2000, I became the dean of academics for a small, independent community college. Its student population was largely nontraditional, consisting of a high percentage of minorities, first-generation students, single parents, and immigrants. In short, these were students whom most of the selective institutions did not want. Being an open admissions community college, our institution usually admitted them.

My first challenge on becoming the dean was to deal with the college's poor retention rate. To address this, I suggested a series of student-support efforts dubbed the Kilian Community College Student Success Initiative. Fundamental to this retention effort was a new mandatory, three-credit course, Introduction to College Studies. In many respects this course was not unlike many offered to freshman students on campuses across the country: a heavy dose of Dave Ellis's *Becoming a Master Student* (2007), some career exploration exercises, and the usual meet-and-greet with college administrative personnel and faculty. Because I had made it clear to the president of the college that I wanted to continue to teach even though I was now the dean, I elected to teach two sections of the new course beginning in fall 2000.

By fall 2003, the Success Initiative was working well, bolstering our retention rates, attracting many new students, and doubling our enrollment. Yet I sensed something was missing, particularly in the course I was teaching. To be sure, we were improving persistence. Students were no longer walking out the back door as fast as they were coming in the front door. The increase in enrollment and retention made the board of trustees happy. So what was missing?

As a community college educator, I had for some time held certain unpopular opinions regarding the focus and mission of America's community colleges. In many instances, a majority of the teaching and learning endeavors was becoming more technical and vocational in nature, with a courtesy nod to the liberal arts in the general education curriculum. In some sense, community colleges have become the great outsource for training future employees. While this is not necessarily a bad thing, it nonetheless begs the question: "Is that all there is?" I remember in the mid-1990s that the majority of prospective new students walking through our doors wanted to be computer programmers. That is where the higher-paying jobs were. So the question was not, "Will this be satisfying life's work? Will being a computer programmer give me meaning and purpose? Is this kind of work suited to who I am?" Rather, the questions were, "How much will I earn? How long will it take to get my degree? Where will I get a job? And why do I have to take algebra?"

About the same time, I was developing my dissertation around the ancient notion of *vocatio*, or calling—that is, being called to a particular life's work. One of the first authors I came across in doing my research was Robert Bellah. In his wonderful book *Habits of the Heart* (1985), Bellah draws distinctions among jobs, careers, and callings. Persons with a calling see no difference between who they are and what they do for work. The two are congruent (Bellah, 1985).

In his little book *Let Your Life Speak: Listening for the Voice of Vocation*, Parker Palmer (2000) suggests that the question, "What am I to do with my life?" is not so important as the questions, "Who am I?" and "What is my nature?" Perhaps this is what I sensed was missing. Both Bellah and Palmer suggested that a contemplation of a life's work should begin with an opportunity for the student to first reflect on "who I am" before considering "what I am going to do."

Matthew Fox's *The Reinvention of Work* (1994) offered another view for consideration: "Work comes from inside out; work is the expression of our soul, our inner being. . . . Work is an expression of the Spirit at work in the world through us" (p. 5). Work as spiritual expression was something I knew was not being discussed anywhere in the curriculum.

In "Career and Calling: Finding a Place for the Spirit in Work and Community," Jon Dalton (2001) provided yet another view about what might be missing:

> The deepest questions in life are spiritual. They are questions about the search for ultimate purposes and enduring truths. They are profoundly personal questions that each of us must ultimately answer in our own way: Who am I? Why am I here? What am I meant for? What is worth living for? How can I be for myself and also for others? Whom and what do I serve? What is it that I love above all else? [p. 17]

These were certainly deeper questions than what I had been having students ponder when considering their life's work. Something significantly important was not being addressed in the course. I had relied mostly on traditional approaches, and in many respects, these approaches seemed to neglect the most important aspect of being human: our spiritual dimension.

At this point, I decided to introduce the notion of *vocatio* into the course. This would enable students to explore those deeper spiritual questions and how they might affect their choice of a life's work. It would give them the opportunity to think seriously about who they were as human beings and how they might choose to be in their world. A life's work, a true vocation, could be an expression of each individual student's own spirit and heart.

NEW DIRECTIONS FOR COMMUNITY COLLEGES • DOI: 10.1002/cc

To guide the student's exploration, I wrote a small book, *Vocatio: Discovering Your Personal Calling* (2005). This was by no means an academic treatise; on the contrary, it was written for students: short chapters, interactive exercises, a compilation of my personal experiences, as well as thoughts ranging from Rumi to Gandhi, Kierkegaard to Carl Rogers. I was more than anxious and filled with trepidation about moving ahead on this new tack.

As one new student had said when she registered for the mandatory course, "Why do I have to take this 'nonsense' course anyway?" My fear was not only that the course would not be seen as valuable by students, but also that the book would be perceived as "nonsense." Besides, although I enjoy writing and sharing ideas, at best, I am only an average wordsmith.

After the first semester, I realized that most students enjoyed the opportunity to discuss and reflect on those deeper questions of life and particularly how they related to choosing a life's work. The following comments were typical responses I received in the students' journals regarding the book:

"I thought this was a fascinating book. This is exactly what should be discussed in college."

"Reading this book really made me stop and think of who I am as a person, what my calling might be, and what I want to do with my life. I really enjoyed reading it and thought it was worth it."

"In many ways this book changed my life. I always thought going to college was about learning so you could make more money. Boy, was I wrong! I found out my life is worth much more than a paycheck."

"My dad said I should go to college to learn accounting. That's what I was going to do until I took this course and read the book. I will make a much better social worker and I think I will be much happier."

"Why didn't any teacher tell me any of this stuff before? My life would have made more sense."

Activities and Exercises

Following is a series of activities and applications I used in the class. I found that the enthusiasm for these varied from class to class, but in the main, the evaluations for this portion of the class were positive.

Journaling.   Journaling was a new experience for most of the students. I believe that journaling can be a spiritual exercise, which is how I introduced it to the students. Before they began to journal, I prefaced the activity by saying that the act of journaling would allow them to reflect on events, concerns, and experiences in their lives. The word *reflection* comes from the Latin word *reflectere*, which means to "bend back." I suggested that when we take time to look back on our day, our life, or our experiences and write down what comes to mind, we are reflecting on those times. When we journal, we are looking for meaning and understanding in those times. I encouraged them to take the time to reflect and write down in their journal pages what they had "seen" and note something they may have discovered about themselves when they were in the actual experience.

I informed them I would keep their journals in strictest confidence. Only I would read them and have access to them. I let them know that journals are private, and since the journals were their very own, they could write anything they wished. At times the journal could also be a type of self-confessional—a place where students could write about their greatest fears, needs, and sorrows. They could even express their mistakes in life and their triumphs. In many ways, a journal kept over time can be a spiritual autobiography.

At the end of each chapter in my book was a perforated journal page that could be turned in at the beginning of class. I read each one and made comments that were positive and encouraging. I made every effort in my comments not to judge or be shocked by what the students had written. Prompts were offered for each journal entry, but the students were not required to answer the prompts. They were more of a means to help students begin to write.

Over the five years I taught the course, I read roughly four thousand journal entries. I was truly amazed at the response. Although some students simply went through the motions to meet the requirement of turning in a journal entry, the majority of the students wrote significant entries. I was always taken by their stories, particularly the ones where the student had experienced tragedy, abuse, or other traumatic events. There were more than a few times I shed tears when reading the journals. While I am convinced this was a useful and beneficial exercise for my students, it also deepened my experience as a teacher, allowing me to know my students in a more profound way and causing me to examine what meaningful teaching entails.

Spiritual Toxins.   This activity was one of my favorites. The first chapter had a quotation from Studs Terkel's book, *Working* (1974): "Work is a search for daily meaning as well as daily bread, for astonishment rather than torpor: in short, for a sort of life rather than a Monday through Friday sort of dying. Perhaps, immortality too, is part of the quest" (p. xi).

I divided the class into groups of four and asked them to read the quotation. Then I asked them to think of a job they had that felt like a "Monday through Friday sort of dying." After that, each person was to write down a list of one-word descriptors of how working at that particular job made it seem like a sort of dying. Finally, they were asked to compare their lists and discuss them with the others in their group. When they finished their discussion, I asked them to compile a list of the descriptors for each of their groups, discarding any duplication.

In the second half of the activity, I asked each group to read their list of descriptors to the class. I wrote each descriptor on the whiteboard at the front of the class in red marker. By the time the last group had reported, the

NEW DIRECTIONS FOR COMMUNITY COLLEGES • DOI: 10.1002/cc

board was usually filled. Students at first found this quite amusing as the descriptors were announced and written on the board. However, when this was finished, I asked them what they thought this might mean.

Responses were varied, and most were not too profound. Finally, I asked them to consider the descriptors once again and asked, "What is this doing to your spirit? How toxic is this to your spiritual health?" This was new ground for most of the students, and good discussion usually followed. Many students would comment on the negative energy that this kind of work produced. Feelings of numbness and even depression were common. Some described anger and resentment. Others spoke of being trapped and feeling hopeless. The discussions usually produced a realization that choosing a life's work needed to be something that nurtured and enhanced their spirit.

The Myers-Briggs Type Indicator. Another activity students enjoyed was taking the Myers-Briggs Type Indicator (MTBI). This personality instrument is one of the older ones available. There are varying opinions on its reliability and validity, but probably no other personality instrument has been researched so much as the MBTI, and the test is continuously revised as a result. If you choose to use the MBTI in your class, you will need to have a trained person administer and interpret the instrument.

Myers-Briggs provides some useful insights to the student's personality, especially as it relates to a life's work. I required only one paper in the course: a reaction paper explaining what the students found out about themselves and what some of the possibilities were that they may have found for their life's work. In addition, students found out how their personalities interacted with other types different from their own. This seemed especially useful in developing a better understanding of family members, coworkers, and significant others.

Several books on the MTBI and spirituality are available. I would have liked to have integrated some more of these into the class. The best book I found for my purposes was *The Four Spiritualities: Expressions of Self, Expression of Spirit* (Richardson, 1996). It introduced students to a broad rendering of the world's more significant spiritual traditions and the spiritual approaches and needs of the sixteen MBTI personality types. However, this work might best be used in a stand-alone course on spiritual formation.

Talking Circles.   The idea for talking circles was suggested to me by a young Sicangu Lakota woman who was a student in the class. She was a fairly traditional Native American and had been raised on the Rosebud Reservation in southwestern South Dakota. Having an affinity for the Lakota people and an interest in their culture, I worked together with her to introduce a talking circle experience in the course. This provided students an encounter with a reflective practice from a different culture. At first, the talking circle appeared to be uncomfortable for students of the dominant culture. The very idea of listening and silence was foreign to them, especially since our lives are so filled with noise of every description.

The talking circle is brought about in this manner. Usually sage is burned at the beginning as part of the rite, but we were not able to do this because of insurance restrictions. The talking circle usually consisted of at least six members, and students were seated on the floor in a circle, an essential form in Native American spirituality. The basic idea of the talking circle is to let everyone say what is in their hearts if they choose to do so. A member is given a feather, and the person who has the feather is allowed to speak about whatever he or she wishes. No one else can talk or interrupt until the person is finished speaking and the feather is passed to the next person in the circle.

There may be long periods of silence as the speaker draws out his or her thoughts. This can make non–Native Americans uncomfortable. Native Americans generally look not at the speaker but down. This is confusing to those of the dominant culture who are taught to look others in the eye when they are talking. However, this is a sign of respect in the Native American culture for the speaker and shows intense listening by the participants in what is being said. Participants never express negative comments about a speaker's thoughts. The feather is passed until everyone has had an opportunity to speak.

Fundamental to the talking circle process is developing the ability to listen and reflect on what is being said. Participants simply let the speaker speak. No feedback is given, which ensures a safe environment. No judgments, advice, or criticism are allowed. A certain spiritual energy evolves that is both cleansing and healing. Although this activity took some time before most of the students were comfortable with it, it succeeded in large part because of the natural generosity, patience, and acceptance of the Native American participants.

Walking by the River.   In many ways, nothing causes us to reflect and contemplate our lives more than interacting with nature. It gives us a perspective on our belonging and acknowledges that we are part of something much greater than our individual selves. In a small way, I tried to provide my students with an activity that would introduce them to that experience. I was reminded of an article I had read by Alicia Chavez (2001), dean of students at the University of Wisconsin, who relates that when she was young, her mother advised her to "go out and walk by the river and think about life" (p. 69). And so that is exactly what my students did.

We were fortunate to have a bike path that ran alongside the river in back of our building. For the activity, I asked the students to walk along the path and contemplate what they were seeing and thinking. I had them walk alone, spacing them out in thirty-second intervals. They were to maintain silence and think about their lives. When each was finished with the walk, I asked them to give me a short feedback on their experience on an index card. The comments ranged over a broad swathe:

NEW DIRECTIONS FOR COMMUNITY COLLEGES • DOI: 10.1002/cc

"Boring."

"I actually saw a mother duck and her babies. I didn't know ducks lived in the river."

"I want to be a muskrat. They just swim around. Not much stress in THEIR lives."

"Surely, there must be some grand design behind all of life."

Once again this was another opportunity for students to reflect on their lives and gain understanding.

These are a few of the activities and exercises I used in the class. There were several others the students did individually that came from my book. I think overall it was a beneficial and enlightening experience for both the students and me. My only regret is that I am no longer teaching.

Conclusion

I have come to several conclusions regarding this type of educational experience.

First, I have little doubt that students hunger for this kind of experience. Time and again in reading the journals, I would read the essential question: "Why haven't I ever heard about all this before?" I believe there is reluctance on the part of administration and faculty to engage students on this level. There are perhaps a number of reasons for this, not the least of which is the prospect of having to come out from behind the comfort and security of the lectern and address the realities in the lives of our students and the questions still unanswered in our own lives.

Second, I am reminded of two observations. The first, by Parker Palmer (1998), concerns how we educate:

> I am equally passionate about not violating the deepest needs of the human soul, which education does with some regularity. As a teacher, I have seen the price we pay for a system of education so fearful of things spiritual that it fails to address the real issues of our lives—dispensing facts at the expense of meaning, information at the expense of wisdom. The price is a school system that alienates and dulls us, that graduates young people, who have had no mentoring in the questions that both enliven and vex the human spirit.

The second comes from Michael Lerner in his book *Spirit Matters* (2000):

> If the goal of education is to ensure your competitive advantage in the marketplace, you will educate in the way that we currently educate. The consequences: huge amounts of unhappiness, a population that has few skills that would make it possible for them to access the richness of a spiritual life, and a society that thinks being rational means being selfish, materialistic and cynical. . . . If your goal is to create a human being who is loving, capable of

showing deep caring for others, alive to the spiritual and ethical dimensions of being, ecologically sensitive, intellectually alive, self determining and creative, there are ways of restructuring education to foster this kind of person [pp. 223–224].

It seems to me that if we are interested in truly being educators, we must continue the discussion of this kind of educational experience. I am always being drawn back to the ancient Latin when seeking the meaning of words. It is unfortunate that some schools no longer teach Latin, for we might better understand what it means to be an educator. *Educo* means to bring forth. How will we bring forth that which is the spiritual dimension in our students?

Third, if you choose to provide this educational experience, be prepared to enter the unknown. There will be many times when you will be asked questions that will cause you to look inside at your own spiritual development. You will not have the comfort of a textbook or an instructor's manual, for these are questions for which you cannot necessarily prepare. Many times the only honest answer is simply, "I don't know. What do you think?"

Here is a caution for you to consider. I inevitably got the question, "What is your religion?" I never reveal this. First, it is not important what my particular religion is to the class. And second, as a semiauthority figure, I do not want my personal beliefs in this area to influence their own spiritual exploration and formation.

Finally, I believe there is a strong need to develop stand-alone classes that provide this kind of educational experience. I understand the concerns of academic administrators and faculty about adding one more course to the curriculum, and it is particularly difficult for community colleges where adding a course such as this requires dropping something else. Four-year institutions may find it easier given that they usually have a larger elective component. Still, it would seem, for the reasons given by Palmer and Lerner, that a course such as this is just as valid as, if even more so than, almost any humanities course.

References

Bellah, R. N. *Habits of the Heart*. New York: HarperCollins, 1985.

Chavez, A. F. "Spirit and Nature in Every Life: Reflections of a Mestiza in Higher Education." In M. A. Jablonski (ed.), *The Implications of Student Spirituality for Student Affairs Practice*. New Directions for Student Services, no. 95. San Francisco: Jossey-Bass, 2001.

Dalton, J. "Career and Calling: Finding a Place for the Spirit in Work and Community." In M. A. Jablonski (ed.), *The Implications of Student Spirituality for Student Affairs Practice*. New Directions for Student Services, no. 95. San Francisco: Jossey-Bass, 2001.

Ellis, D. *Becoming a Master Student*. 12th ed. Boston: Houghton Mifflin, 2007.

Fox, M. *The Reinvention of Work: A New Vision of Livelihood for Our Time.* San Francisco: HarperCollins, 1994.

Lerner, M. *Spirit Matters.* Charlottesville, Va.: Hampton Roads Publishing, 2000.

Palmer, P. J. "Evoking the Spirit in Public Education." *Educational Leadership,* 1998, 56(3), 6–11. Retrieved July 20, 2010, from http://www.couragerenewal.org/parker/writings/evoking-the-spirit.

Palmer, P. J. *Let Your Life Speak: Listening for the Voice of Vocation.* San Francisco: Jossey-Bass, 2000.

Richardson, P.T. *The Four Spiritualities: Expressions of Self, Expression of Spirit.* Boston: Intercultural Press, 1996.

Scott, C. F. *Vocatio: Discovering Your Personal Calling.* Sioux Falls, S. Dak.: Pine Hill Press, 2005.

Terkel, S. *Working.* New York: Pantheon, 1974.

CLIFFORD "KIP" SCOTT *consults with community colleges and served as dean of academic services at Kilian Community College in Sioux Falls, South Dakota.*

NEW DIRECTIONS FOR COMMUNITY COLLEGES • DOI: 10.1002/cc

This chapter offers a brief overview of the contemplative practices discussed in the volume.

Contemplative Practice in the Classroom

Keith Kroll

This volume has offered both the theory and practice for a model of contemplative teaching and learning in community colleges—a way of teaching, of learning, of thinking that has often been missing in higher education. Contemplative teaching and learning, with its focus on community, reflection, and mindfulness—in short, on what it means to be human—is a complement to the objective and data-driven education that has a strong foundation and tradition in higher education.

To give readers a place to begin their own contemplative practices in the classroom, the balance of this chapter summarizes the contemplative practices discussed throughout the volume, along with the numbers of the chapters that discuss the contemplative practice.

The Classroom as *Sangha*

- Almost any classroom activity may be transformed into a contemplative one simply by treating it the way the contemplative art teacher treats a slide in art class: slowing the activity long enough to "behold"—to facilitate deep attention to and intimate familiarity with—the object of study, whether it is a slide, textual passage, equation, claim, or argument. (Chapter One)
- Create downtime that is unstructured, unplanned, and open to discovery. (Chapters Two, Three, Four, and Nine)
- Place fewer subjects before students, and allow them to go deeper into each one. (Chapters Two and Three)

New Directions for Community Colleges, no. 151, Fall 2010 © 2010 Wiley Periodicals, Inc.
Published online in Wiley Online Library (wileyonlinelibrary.com) • DOI: 10.1002/cc.420

- Use fewer certainties and more healthy uncertainty to invite the search for lifelong learning. (Chapters Two and Three)
- Students and their teachers can gather themselves as a class by sitting together for even five or ten minutes in silence. (Chapters Two through Four, and Chapter Nine)

Mindfulness Meditation

- Begin any class with a simple exercise in mindfulness (nonconcentrative, nonjudgmental awareness) or pointedness (concentrative focus on any single item of experience). Such an exercise promises to help sustain an attitude of beholding, in both students and faculty, throughout what follows. (Chapters Two through Seven)
- One-pointedness meditation involves concentrative focus on a single item of experience, such as focusing attention on the flow of breath in and out of the nostrils, listening to a particular sound, or gazing at a candle flame. (Chapters Three and Four)

Writing

- Make time for "aha" papers that capture a moment of realization or shift in perception, with time for questions like, "What questions remain?" (Chapter Two)
- Freewriting in a journal at the start of class sessions offers an excellent means to infuse a reflective element into any course, regardless of subject matter. (Chapters Three, Five, and Six)
- Journaling that encourages students to reflect on the events of their lives. (Chapters Six and Nine)

Reading

- Practice reflective reading in the classroom. Students might linger over a few sentences by Emerson, Thoreau, Wendell Berry, or Barry Lopez or over a few lines by Whitman, Shakespeare, Wang Wei, or W. S. Merwin. The idea is not to extract meaning from the passage so much as to allow meaning to accumulate with the passage. (Chapters Two, Three, Five, and Nine)
- Students walk around with a passage, read it over and over through the day, and observe it from numerous perspectives. Like the newly rediscovered joy and meaning of slow food, students can find the richness and enjoyment of slow reading. (Chapter Three)

NEW DIRECTIONS FOR COMMUNITY COLLEGES • DOI: 10.1002/cc

Campuswide Professional Development

• Offer faculty and staff a professional development model using "'formation, a type of reflective practice," based on the "Circle of Trust" as described in the work of Parker Palmer. (Chapter Eight)

KEITH KROLL *teaches in the English Department at Kalamazoo Valley Community College in Kalamazoo, Michigan.*

INDEX

ORDER FORM SUBSCRIPTION AND SINGLE ISSUES

DISCOUNTED BACK ISSUES:

Use this form to receive 20% off all back issues of *New Directions for Community College*.
All single issues priced at **$23.20** (normally $29.00)

TITLE	ISSUE NO.	ISBN

*Call 888-378-2537 or see mailing instructions below. When calling, mention the promotional code JBNND
to receive your discount. For a complete list of issues, please visit www.josseybass.com/go/ndcc*

SUBSCRIPTIONS: (1 YEAR, 4 ISSUES)

☐ New Order   ☐ Renewal

U.S.	☐ Individual: $89	☐ Institutional: $259
CANADA/MEXICO	☐ Individual: $89	☐ Institutional: $299
ALL OTHERS	☐ Individual: $113	☐ Institutional: $333

*Call 888-378-2537 or see mailing and pricing instructions below.
Online subscriptions are available at www.onlinelibrary.wiley.com*

ORDER TOTALS:

Issue / Subscription Amount: $ _____

Shipping Amount: $ _____
(for single issues only – subscription prices include shipping)

Total Amount: $ _____

SHIPPING CHARGES:

First Item $5.00
Each Add'l Item $3.00

*(No sales tax for U.S. subscriptions. Canadian residents, add GST for subscription orders. Individual rate subscriptions must
be paid by personal check or credit card. Individual rate subscriptions may not be resold as library copies.)*

BILLING & SHIPPING INFORMATION:

☐ **PAYMENT ENCLOSED:** *(U.S. check or money order only. All payments must be in U.S. dollars.)*

☐ **CREDIT CARD:**   ☐VISA ☐MC ☐AMEX

Card number _____Exp. Date_____

Card Holder Name_____Card Issue #_____

Signature _____Day Phone_____

☐ **BILL ME:** *(U.S. institutional orders only. Purchase order required.)*

Purchase order #_____
Federal Tax ID 13559302 • GST 89102-8052

Name_____

Address_____

Phone_____ E-mail_____

Copy or detach page and send to: **John Wiley & Sons, PTSC, 5th Floor
989 Market Street, San Francisco, CA 94103-1741**

Order Form can also be faxed to: **888-481-2665**

PROMO JBNND